Beyond the Bake Sale
The Ultimate School Fund-Raising Book

Second Edition WITHDRAWN

Jean C. Joachim

Moonlight Books, New York, NY

D1450870

INTRODUCTION

This step-by-step guide provides you with the tools to create a fund-raising program to suit your school or organization. Realistic goals, specific information, including websites, timelines, and secrets for success are laid out here in easy-to-follow instructions. For schools new to fund-raising, there is a "just starting out" section for each event.

Though much has changed in this second edition, one thing has remained the same –the importance of fund-raising for parent associations and the need for more funds for schools.

Fund-raising at PS 261 supported the goals of the school and also built community. Fund-raising connected students, staff, families, and the broader community. Parents worked hard to identify strategies for raising money that would ultimately support their children's education and be inclusive of all constituents in the school community. Funds would be earmarked that aligned closely with the instructional goals of the school. The school community worked diligently to ensure that there was equity and that all students benefited from the funds that were raised.

JUDI ARONSON
RETIRED PRINCIPAL OF P.S. 261
BROOKLYN, NY

A successful school creates and nurtures a sense of community that encourages a collaborative effort on the part of all its constituencies toward the ultimate desired outcome of the development of intellectually capable, well-prepared, and confident students and contributors to society. At. P.S. 87, fund-raising plays an important role in achieving this goal.

STEVEN PLAUT,
FORMER PRINCPAL AT P.S .87

ABOUT THE AUTHOR

Jean C. Joachim, parent of two sons, spent sixteen years as a board member of the parents associations of New York City elementary, middle, and high schools. Naturally drawn to fund-raising, she participated in many committees and chaired a few as well.

In each school, Jean was part of a team that created ground-breaking fund-raising events. It wasn't long before fund-raising captured her heart. It wasn't about the money but the sense of community it built within the school and among the parents, teachers, administrators, and students. Besides, it was a lot of fun.

She believes her efforts to help her sons' schools impacted their lives in a positive way and supported students who would otherwise have been left wanting.

This second edition to her first book on fund-raising has been crafted with the same intention as the first book—to share what she's learned through the years with schools around the world.

TABLE OF CONTENTS

DEDICATION

For all the parents of students in public and
private schools.

ACKNOWLEDGMENTS
Many thanks to the parents and staff at P.S. 87, Delta, and Brooklyn
Technical High School for their insight, wisdom, energy and support

THE BASICS

"At 87, fund-raising has been elevated to an art that connects students, families, and staff. Fund-raising at P.S. 87 serves as a community builder. It brings together families and staff and provides vehicles for parents to be part of and contribute to their children's education. A clearly articulated vision of the goals of fund-raising, as well as accountability and demonstrated evidence of how the proceeds both directly and indirectly benefit students, is at the core of the program."

STEVEN PLAUT,
FORMER PRINCIPAL AT P.S. 87

The fund-raising events and activities in this book reflect years of experience creating events, making money, and saving money. We made plenty of mistakes in our fund-raising efforts, but we never got discouraged. I learned that it takes a year or two to get an event to run smoothly. You have to have patience, be creative, listen to other people, and be open to suggestions.

If you are just starting out, your school or parents association (PA) may not have much cash. Some of the events described in this book require money to pay for things upfront, like food or a rental hall for your auction. In each chapter that has an event or activity requiring a significant outlay of cash, I created a special section at the end called "Just Starting Out?" This section outlines ways to start the event without much money.

We have stripped the event down to the basics to get it going. As your financial reserves grow, you can add on any of the more costly activities.

A RESERVE FUND

I can't stress enough the importance of putting some of your profits aside to form a reserve fund. Back in the day, we created a healthy reserve fund over the years. There have been times when we had to dip into that fund and were so grateful it was there. And when we did dip in, we worked hard to replace the money.

A reserve fund is essential to any fund-raising plan that is going to grow and be a stable source of funds for school improvement year in and year out.

If you save half the money your parents association earns, you will quickly build a reserve fund. Plan to have a year's budget in reserve. If you're budgeting to take in $10,000, your goal for a reserve fund would be the same—$10,000

You can accomplish this by budgeting to spend only half of what you make. Put the other half in a special fund that earns interest so the money will grow over time.

If you need more money during the year, have a quick and easy fund-raiser, like a bake sale, instead of dipping into the funds you have put away. This is the only way you will have enough money to throw a major event that requires a significant cash outlay. Save your money for a rainy day and build your financial power.

GET THE BASICS BEFORE YOU START FUND-RAISING

Successful school fund-raising requires solid support systems, like:

1. a widely-read PA newsletter sent to parents;
2. good relationships with the teachers and the administrative staff, including the secretaries and other support staff in the office;
3. active, reliable class parents;
4. a school handbook spelling out dates and regular fund-raising events for the year;
5. an up-to-date school phone and email directory; and a PA or

parents association website.

SCHOOL NEWSLETTER

Start with a four-page paper newsletter (11" x 17" folded once) stuffed into students' backpacks and emailed.

Instead of paper, an email newsletter may be the way to go.

Take a survey and see which the parents prefer. It's possible you will have parents who do not have access to email. If that's so, then you will have to print newsletters for them. Ask your school to help by allowing the PA to print on school equipment. The PA can provide the paper.

To get a newsletter in the hands of middle school and high school parents, you'll have to either mail a printed newsletter or send one via email. Older students won't take home a paper newsletter, and since parents no longer pick their children up, you can't hand them one.

Hopefully, middle and high school parents will have email addresses, so you won't have the expense of mailing.

TIP: If you do a paper newsletter, consider printing it on colored paper. This will make it stand out but not cost as much as color printing.

How often should you send a newsletter? With schedules tight and free time at a minimum for parents, send only once a week. What to include in your newsletter? Here are a few suggestions:

- principal's column
- parents association president's column
- schedule of upcoming events
- classified ads

Note to high schools: If you can get a schedule from guidance counselors when college representatives will be visiting the school, that would be valuable to include in your newsletter. You might also want to include the schedule of athletic competitions—for example, which football team your school is playing or when the next track meet will take place.

This invaluable tool is important for publicity for upcoming fundraising events. Use your newsletter to recruit and thank volunteers, publish the success of your events, request donations, and keep parents abreast of the changes in the school.

It's a big job to get the newsletter set up. But once you have settled on a format, font style, basic departments, and a logo, it's not so difficult.

Consider putting together a stable of different people to construct your newsletter . Every week place a special packet folder in the school office for newsletter submissions. The editor in charge of that week picks up the folder on Thursday afternoon.

Prefer to use the Internet? Designate a special email address for newsletter submissions. That makes it so easy to send those off to an editor.

If you can get ten people with computer access to agree to type and edit one month's editions of the newsletter, you'll have the year covered.

Sell sponsorships. Local businesses, even parents in the school, might sponsor a newsletter. Sponsorship should cover the cost of printing the newsletter. Sponsors should receive acknowledgment and a 3" x 4" ad. If you get sponsors, then it will not cost anything to print and distribute.

Some likely places to find sponsors are: summer camps, real estate brokers, insurance agents, the local hardware store, or even a pizza shop, especially if they're advertising a special deal.

For a reasonable sum, a business can reach hundreds of families by advertising in the local school newsletter. If you can sign up sponsors at the beginning of the year, you can easily run a cost-efficient newsletter.

In the school office every Monday morning, a parent volunteer counts out the correct number of copies for each class and puts them in the teachers' mailboxes. The teachers distribute the newsletters to the kids to take home every Tuesday. The deadline for submissions is Thursday if handing in on paper, or Friday by email (since it doesn't have to be typed in).

Classified ads also generate income. They are free to all parents with children in the school. Help-wanted ads are also accepted free of charge. Nonparent classified advertisers pay $25 per ad, but teachers can run classified ads for free—another teacher perk. Ad length is determined by space availability, a decision determined by the editor of the week.

A PA WEBSITE

A PA website is extremely valuable as a tool to disseminate information. Find a tech-savvy parent in the school who can construct the school website for free. Some teachers may want to post their homework assignments on

the website. That way, if children are absent or their memories are unreliable, the parents can access the homework assignments and make sure the children are getting them all completed on time.

Here are a few ideas about what to post:

- The PA newsletter
- Pictures of events, such as a talent show or science fair, to inspire people to volunteer
- The school art show.

- Email address for each teacher and administrator.
- School calendar, which includes holidays.
- Testing schedule.
- PTA meetings and events calendar by month.
- PTA board members email/contact information.
- With a special password for parents only, you can post PA budgets.
- Teacher wish lists.
- Kid's book recommendations by the school librarian.

GOOD RELATIONSHIPS WITH TEACHERS

Our parents association made it a point to support and acknowledge teachers. The teachers are the lifeblood of your school. Teachers' help with fund-raising is vital. It's the teachers, not the parents, who hand out the forms and information for your wrapping-paper and magazine drives. In fact, it is the elementary school teachers who:

- collect fund-raising forms
- create class projects for the auction
- create class booths for the street fair
- create a quilt to be sold at the auction
- offer to take children out for breakfast or pizza as an auction prize

- bring their classes down to bake sales and book fairs
- disseminate the newsletter every week

And, of course, in addition to those and a thousand other things, they teach your children. You should do everything you can for the teachers. On parent/teacher conference nights, throw a potluck dinner just for the teachers. In the evenings, the teachers are too busy with conferences to go out for a meal. Serve delicious, homemade food in the cafeteria so the teachers don't have to go hungry.

P.S. 87 gave free tickets to the auction to the teachers. Many teachers prefer to stay home with their own families than to spend Saturday night with the parents of the kids in their class, but still, the gesture is warm and inclusive.

Make classified ads free for teachers.

P.S. 87 earmarked funds for every teacher. This money was divided up by levels:

- Returning teachers: $200
- New teachers: $400

- Teachers changing grades: $300

The teachers decide how to spend the money. Receipts are required for each expense. All expenses are submitted to the treasurer for approval.

Once in a while you might get a special request from a teacher, like a special poetry or art book created by a teacher with participation open to all students of all grades. If a teacher gets a grant that falls short of finishing the project, the PA might step in and pay the additional expenses.

Ask teachers for wish lists. At P.S. 87, teachers needs ran the gamut from supplies to furniture, from appliances to books for the classroom. Host an appreciation breakfast for teachers every year.

A good relationship between the PA board and the teachers is essential. Ask you board to come up with eight ideas for showing teacher appreciation. Pick two or three and make them happen. After all, everything we do is about supporting the classroom, the teachers, and creating the best school experience possible for our children.

The same attitude holds true for the administrative support staff in the office. I don't know how many times I needed help from the office administrative staff, and they have been there every time.

From opening the locked PA closet door, to copying, to helping me locate a teacher, a child, or a parent, not to mention letting the PA keep all kinds of flyers, newsletters, and auction donation forms, in the office—the office staff has been vital to our success. Auction and streetfair donations get dropped off there, too.

It is impossible to stress enough the importance of having the office staff at your side. Make it clear you appreciate them. Buy them a cup of coffee, a doughnut or flowers now and then. Remember to say please and thank you.

CLASS PARENTS

Class parents are parents who volunteer to be responsible for parents association communication with other parents in their child's class. I recommend two class parents per class so one can back up the other. They are essential to successful school fund-raising. Class parents help with field trips, straighten up in the classroom, and coordinate collecting for the teacher gifts at holiday time and the end of the year, too.

But class parents are also an important part of school fund-raising because they represent personal communication. Class parents call other parents or speak with them face-to-face at play dates, morning drop-off, or afternoon pickup at school. Class parents enable the school fund-raising efforts to reach right into each classroom to pull volunteers or donations and generate activity.

Class parents become part of the parent network. Usually, the teacher selects two parents who volunteered from his or her class to become the class parents. These people are responsible for making sure the school fund-raising is being supported in their class. They are the ones who decide, frequently in collaboration with the teacher, what the class booth at the street fair will be. The class parents are the ones who contact the parents in their child's

class and urge people to donate to the auction or contribute to the pledge drive. The class parents are the ones pushing the wrapping-paper sales and magazine drive. The class parents make sure the teacher gets a book wish list to Book Fairs. They tidy up students for school photos.

Class parents create a phone tree by dividing their class list into four or five columns and listing people vertically. Then the class parent calls each parent at the top of a column, and each parent then calls the parent beneath him or her on the phone tree with the same message. Using a phone tree means that every parent, with the exception of the class parent, only has to make one phone call and everyone in the class is reached quickly and efficiently.

STAFF RELATIONS

Successful school fund-raising requires the help of the school staff. From administrators to custodians, you will need everyone to pitch in. Go out of your way to build bridges.

Acknowledge and reward the school staff.

I can't run a bake sale if the custodian doesn't get the big tables set up and the extension cord for the coffee machine in place. I'm stuck if he doesn't bring the giant garbage cans with lots of extra bags for my rummage sale. Many cooperative teachers have let us use classrooms to make coffee or store excess stuff. Office staff members have made copies and kept track of deliveries. Remember, without the support of the principal and assistant principals, you won't be able to do anything in the school at all. You will need all the support you can get.

HANDBOOKS

There are three kinds of handbooks that will help you with fund-raising: a parent or school handbook, a new-teacher handbook, and a community resource handbook.

PARENT/SCHOOL HANDBOOK

This handbook is a collaboration between the administration and the parents association. A good handbook should inform the parents of all the rules and regulations regarding their child's new school. In addition to the basics like admonishing the parents to bring their children to school on time, the handbook also outlines the fund-raisers planned for the school year. You will need only two people to create the handbook: one who knows the school inside out and one who can type. They can even be the same person. Once a handbook is produced, it can be used for years with only minor changes.

Either the PA or the school can print the handbook and distribute it free to the new parents. Distribute it to new teachers, too, to get them acquainted with your activities early in the year. PS 87 printed theirs on three-hole paper so

parents can keep it in a binder. You can make the handbook whatever you want it to be. Here is a place to start:

1. A mission statement. Get the mission statement from your principal or assistant principal. If you have a school leadership team, you can get this from them.
2. Add a paragraph about your school, including your logo and slogan, if you have one.
3. A section on admissions, physical exams, list of all types of staff (by position rather than by name).
4. A resources and facilities section, including a floor plan of the school, highlighting the locations of the school restrooms and which ones are available for parents versus students only. This section includes brief descriptions of:

- Library
- Science Resource Center (if you have one)
- Garden
- Or any other special area your school might have.

These sections set up some of the special facilities the PA provides so when donations are requested, people already have some idea where the money they contribute might go.

1. A curriculum section, by grade, provided by teachers and approved by the administration.
2. A brief section on kindergarten, including the orientation period and a description of a typical day to help make the new kindergarten parents feel more at ease.
3. A section on assessment, standardized testing, and frequently asked questions zeros in on parents' common concerns.
4. The parents association section, which starts with the PA board, school-wide committees, and finally fund-raising.

- This chapter gives a brief overview of the annual fund-raising events and the month or season they take place and includes year-round fund-raising activities, too.

- Teacher and parents association wish lists
- The flea market
- A pie chart showing the distribution of PA funds

- Parent Network Committee
- Class Parents
- After-school program—Needed is a brief description of your after-school programs.
- School rules.

COMMUNITY RESOURCE HANDBOOK

The Community Resource Handbook began with questionnaires to incoming kindergarten parents about their skills, jobs, and hobbies. Soon, it became apparent the PA needed the resources of all the parents in the school. So a questionnaire was created

to gather information about abilities, experiences,

professions, and hobbies and was distributed to all the parents in the school.

A handbook was compiled from the questionnaires, dividing parents into groups, like music, marketing, carpentry, writing, police, sewing, covering the diverse skills of the parents. The handbook was distributed to the teachers and put in the library. The teachers had a ready reference of whom to contact if they needed a bookshelf built or a short lecture to the class on the stock market.

The book was extremely popular and became a resource for fundraising, too. With this book, you can locate parents who have lighting experiences to help with your haunted house, or who work for the Fortune 500 companies if you need a specific donation, or who are professional actors to perform as storybook characters for your street fair.

Put your questionnaire in the first issue of your newsletter. Form a committee to gather this information and publish a community resource handbook.

THE SCHOOL DIRECTORY

It's impossible to run successful school fund-raising without this tool. The school directory should list all the students by class, with alphabetical cross-referenced listings in the back.

We listed a cross-reference with parents who have different last names from their children in the back, too.

We also listed all the names of the members of the PA board, their phone numbers, and e-mail addresses. We listed all the important numbers for the school, like the office, the guidance counselors, and the nurse.

We sold advertising in the directory to cut down on the printing cost and so were able to distribute the directory free to all families. Consider charging a dollar for a second copy.

The directory is where everyone goes to call for volunteers or donations. In addition, you can't manage your child's social life without it. The biggest problem with the school directory is getting it out quickly.

To get your directory out at the earliest possible date, start gathering the information at the end of the year. Get next year's classes from administration and begin the directory during the summer. In the fall, you'll just have to add kindergarten classes, a few new students in other grades, and make a handful of class changes. This will speed up delivery of the directory.

PHONE TREES

A phone tree is a class list broken up into columns of names. You can usually fit four columns on a page. Each column has a student and parent lined up underneath. Then the person at the top of the column calls the parent directly underneath to pass along information, ask for volunteering, or for, donations. Then that person makes one phone call to the person underneath her name, and so on. Eventually, everyone on the list gets called and each person only had to make one phone call. Here is what it looks like:

Edna Brown
146 Chestnut Street
Edison, NC
Mary Brown
Kevin Brown
344-7988
Gary Barrett
422 Elm Street
Rhonda Barrett
Glen Barrett
324-6659
Once you have these support systems in place, you're ready to begin planning your first fund-raising events.

* * * *

"Eagerly awaited events such as the magazine drive in the fall the auction in late winter, and the "Just Kids Street Fair" in the spring, to name but a few, mark the passage of the school year as surely as any academic calendar. The benefits that accrue to the students transcend the material improvements to their school. Children develop an appreciation for the priority that education represents for their families as well as perceiving their school as a community that is the basis of the formation of lifelong relationships and friendships."

STEVEN PLAUT,
FORMER P.S. 87 PRINCIPAL

FALL EVENT

The Pledge Drive

WHAT IS A PLEDGE DRIVE?

A pledge drive is a plea for money—like your local radio station does or the Public Broadcasting Television station in your area holds at least once a year. The school pledge drive doesn't use broadcast media, it arrives through the mail or by email, instead. During broadcast telethons, people pledge, or promise, to donate a specific amount of money to be sent in at a later date. Your school pledge drive letter should ask for an immediate donation to your parents association by check, money order, or credit card. There are two ways to run a pledge drive: mail through the post office and email.

HOW DOES A SCHOOL PLEDGE DRIVE WORK?

1. The old-fashioned way, through the post office

Mail a letter from the parents' association president to parents asking for donations of money. Describe what the funds will be used for and how money has been spent in the

past. You can ask for a specific amount. One elementary school in my neighborhood asks for $300. If you choose to do the same, pick an amount that isn't too high or too low for the parents in your school.

Get the best copywriter parent volunteer you can to write the solicitation letter. The letter should explain why the money is needed and specifically where the money will go. At P.S. 87, we used a pie chart to show what percentage of our fund-raising went to each program. Usually, it was 33 percent to the library, 20 percent to the art program, five percent to science enrichment, and so on. Mail the pledge drive letter along with the summer mailing from your school so the school, instead of the parents association, picks up the postage. If your school doesn't do a summer mailing, perhaps you can encourage them to start one.

Can you do a special letter to kindergarten parents? A welcoming letter explaining some about the school and asking for a donation would help increase donations from those parents.

Enclose an addressed reply envelope in your mailing. It doesn't need to be postage paid. The reply envelope will increase response and ensure that it goes to the right person at the correct address. Pledge drive money goes to the treasurer. But, if the treasurer is on vacation in August whenthe replies start coming in, have the donations sent to the PA president or another responsible board member.

Ask people to give what they can. Public school parents typically come at all the income levels. Be sure your letter is not too demanding and does not make lower-income parents in your school feel badly if they can't afford to contribute much or at all. Point out that there are many ways to contribute, such as donating time to run a class booth at the street fair or donating a cake, cookies, or brownies to a bake sale.

Downside: unless you can ride along with a school mailing, postage and printing are expensive. If you're just starting out, you might not have enough money. See below for sending an email pledge drive letter.

Also, the letter has to be generic, appropriate for all age groups and all grade. This means that you can't target one grade over another by highlighting specific programs geared only for one grade over another. The programs you mention that need funds should be ones that affect the whole school, like the library, music, sports, and art programs.

1. Email pledge letter

Emailing a pledge letter is easier and cheaper.
There are two ways to do this.

- Attach a Word document/letter to an email.

- Include the letter in the body of the email.

Many people are wary of opening attachments, so if you can put the letter in the body of the email, you're more likely to get your email opened—first hurdle in pledge drive efforts. If you have an email list from the year before, you can adapt that for the coming year by moving all the families up to the next grade.

You will have to get the email addresses of the incoming kindergarten parents from the school. Hopefully, the principal will understand and help you out. One of the benefits of doing an email campaign is that you can tailor each letter to the grade. For example, if you're raising money for scholarships to fourth grade Nature Camp, you can mention that as a goal in your email letter to fourth grade parents. The more you tie your goals to the grade of the student whose parents you're emailing, the more likely you are to get a contribution.

Keep it short. Downside of email: You may have to use a service to send out all the letters, unless the school does it for you. Some people won't open the email.

Upside: it doesn't cost anything to send it. You can put a "donate now" link right in the letter. That will increase the number of responses and the amounts of the donations.

IMPORTANT LINK: Sign up for free for a nonprofit donation link at:

https://www.paypal.com/us/webapps/mpp/donations

PayPal is a trusted, well-known site that has been around for a long time. There is no upfront cost to getting an account with them for your school. They take only 2.2% of the donation and a $.30 fee for each donation. There is no monthly fee.

A PayPal donation account will eliminate the hassle and charges of bounced checks.

VOLUNTEERS

This event brings in the most money with the least number of volunteers. Volunteers for the pledge drive must be able to work during the summer as the first mailing goes out in August. You need only a chairperson and about three volunteers including the treasurer, to:

- write copy
- have the letter copied and order the envelopes or set up the email, if you choose that method.
- get the mailing out (get help from school staff)
- keep track of and post response

SECRETS TO INCREASING PLEDGE DRIVE REVENUE

Maximize your revenue by offering the option of paying through PayPal which takes credit cards. You may increase donations as much as three times through PayPal.

Or get your own credit card account. Since you are already a 501c3 nonprofit organization, you should be able to get help from your bank in securing a business credit card account. The fees may be higher than PayPal. Get the facts before you decide.

TIP: Offer a payment plan where the parent donor's credit card is charged a specific amount indicated by the parent each month for three to six months. If a parent wanted to donate $300, but not all at once, *you could be authorized to charge their credit card $50 per month for six months.*

Installment payments like that make it easier for some parents to give more money. Credit cards cut down on bounced checks, too, saving your PA time trying to get those checks made good and saving the high cost of returned-check charges from the bank.

1. Timing

Timing matters. Rather than mail during the year-end, when most nonprofits seek funds—so people can deduct it from their income tax—mail right before the school year begins – for two reasons:

- A December mailing gets lost amid holiday cards, other pledge drive requests from major companies, and the deluge of holiday catalogs emailing every day.
- You can highlight the projects earmarked for their funds before the school year begins. Parents will see they are helping to make things happen right now, as the school year begins. Cash in on the enthusiasm of parents as they face a new school year with their children. Making this switch to an August 15 mailing date boosted the amount of money received at P.S. 87 by almost three times over what we collected in December.

Mailing early while people are excited about and anticipating a new school year is key. Get contributions from parents before they become disenchanted with their child's teacher or something else occurs that might turn them off the idea of donating money. Mail or email early to new kindergarten parents who have gotten used to paying huge preschool fees. A one-time contribution of $300 may seem paltry to people who have been paying $500 or more per month for preschool.

1. Ask for a specific donation amount.

If every family were able to donate $300, we wouldn't have had to do any additional fund-raising at all. Of course, we didn't get $300 per family, as there are many families in our community who couldn't afford to donate even $50. But we got enough from those who could donate to push our pledge drive up and up.

1. **Make a connection with new families before they enter school.**

Divide up a list of new parents for the PA board members to contact before the school year begins. Welcome them with personal letters or phone calls from board members and a picnic just for new parents, board members, and their children. Welcoming new parents helps reduce their September anxiety by making them feel like a part of your special community even before they walk in the door.

Kindergarten is more daunting to the student's family than people realize. New parents may feel overwhelmed by the size of your school and the tight-knit PA. A friendly hand extended before the year begins helps make them more comfortable right away. You may see this warm greeting reflected in donations to your pledge drive from new parents.

A new parent breakfast in the schoolyard on the first two morning of school gives parents the opportunity to hear from members of the PA board, meet experienced parents, and ask questions. The breakfasts help these parents make the adjustment to "real" school from preschool.

Add sign-up sheets for PA committees, from library to technology to fund-raising, to capture volunteers early. This provides an opportunity to get parents, who will be in the school for six years, involved and volunteering early on.

1. **Incentives.**

Publicize your success. You might want to keep a running bar graph in the school lobby showing which class or grade has raised the most money through the pledge drive. Consider publishing a list of the names of donors, but not the amount donated, in the school lobby. Throw a pizza or ice cream party for the class whose parents donated the most money. Think of simple but public incentives that could work in your school.

1. Write thank-you notes.

This job should be the responsibility of the administrative vice president or the secretary of the PA board. Thank-you notes are an excellent way to acknowledge donations and make new parents feel appreciated right away. Handwritten is best, but if you don't have time, use a printed card with real signatures and a word or two. Timeliness is important.

1. Email again.

The same pledge drive letter can be emailed again can produce more donations. Or write a new letter telling your parents how much you still need to raise to meet your goal. Don't email the second letter until the end of October to give parents time to respond to the first letter. Be sure to email before Thanksgiving. You don't want parents' generosity to be short-circuited by the financial burdens of the upcoming holidays.

1. Have a table at parent/teacher conference night.

Set up a table or desk manned by a volunteer and a sign to collect pledge drive money anyone wants to give on the spot. Be prepared to take credit cards at that table, too. This is ideal as you have all the parents in the school marching in and out during conference.

HOW MUCH MONEY WILL YOU RAISE?

It is hard to predict the response to the pledge drive. The pledge drive funds raised may fluctuate because of economic conditions as well as the mix of families in your school. Whatever you raise through a pledge drive is usually considered gravy since it didn't involve much in the way of volunteers or time compared to many other events. Back in the day, our best year produced over $85,000. But that's from a big school of almost 1,000 students. Results may vary from year to year, too.

TIMELINE

Beginning of June (end of the year)

Find a copywriter.

Obtain list of next year's incoming parents' email or snail mail addresses.

Middle to end of June

Finalize copy.

Order printed reply envelopes, get letter copied—if you are doing snail mail. Get thank-you notes ready.

July

Add letters and reply envelopes to the school mailing.

August

Mail—either through the post office or via email.

Donations should begin to arrive.

Beginning of October

Mail a second letter stressing how close you are to your goal and how much more is needed.

The Wrapping Paper Drive

WHAT IS A WRAPPING PAPER DRIVE?

Several companies have programs that give schools or parents associations a percentage of the revenue from sales made through the school. My school sold wrapping paper with varying results. This is an easy fund-raising and doesn't require the school to lay out a dime. Some companies offering wrapping paper fund-raisers are:

Charleston Wrap

https://www.charlestonwrap.com/school-fundraising-programs/

Genevieve's

https://www.genevieves.com/

Resource Solutions

www.resourcefundraising.com[1]

The company prepares everything you need to run a successful wrapping paper drive, including a catalog, often with actual paper samples and order forms. It is important to stress that the children should not be out selling wrapping paper door-to-door by themselves, for safety reasons. A parent or another responsible adult should always accompany children.

Each company works in its own way. Select the company with the right product mix for your school population and the highest percentage of sales donated to the school. Make sure the company has an easy-to-follow bookkeeping procedure for this fund-raiser. Volunteers will be handling this.

You can offer more than just wrapping paper. Genevieve's and Resource Solutions offer more than just wrapping paper. There will be more work for the volunteers as you'll have more than one catalog, more choices, and additional forms to fill out, depending on how many catalogs you use. The chairperson must keep orders straight.

---

1.   http://www.resourcefundraising.com

You might want to start with just one catalog and one product or a catalog combining wrapping paper with other holiday gift items might work best at your school. Speak with different companies and pick the combination of items you think will work best with your parent body.

The company will send you all the catalogs and forms you need. Remember to ask for extra catalogs. There will always be a few parents who lose the catalog or want to give one to "Aunt Martha" to sell to her office staff, so order about 10% more than your school population.

Offices are a great place to make multiple sales easily. Be sure to suggest that your parents tap their colleagues to benefit your school.

HOW DOES THE WRAPPING PAPER DRIVE WORK?

The chairperson or persons and two or three volunteers get together and count out the proper number of catalogs for each classroom. A volunteer delivers the catalogs to the classrooms.

Teachers disseminate the catalogs and collect the orders.

When the orders start coming in, the teacher can put them in a plastic bag and hang it on the outside knob of the classroom door or you can have a box in the office where teachers can deposit order forms.

Hanging a bag of orders on the classroom door allows the chair or other volunteers to pick up the orders without disturbing the class.

Some people don't want to send orders in with young children. Instruct them, through a notice in your school newsletter or a separate email, to drop orders in the office. It's easy to collect late orders from a box in the school office, too. Put a sign on the school front and back doors.

A group of volunteers processes the orders as they come in. Start right away. If you wait until they are all in, you'll be inundated. Starting early gives you time to gather information missing from order forms before you're snowed under with orders.

Allow four weeks for this process from start to finish. About a month or more after you have completed all the paperwork and sent the check to the wrapping paper company, the wrapping paper is delivered. The company should send each order complete and already boxed so you don't have to do anything but distribute it.

Inform parents the wrapping paper has arrived. Use your newsletter and signs around the school. Because you will need a lot of space, keep the orders in the gymnasium or on the stage in the auditorium.

The parents or caregivers must come and pick up their orders since many orders are too heavy for children to carry home on their own.

Volunteers check off each order as they pick it up. Do not have more than three or four people handling this job since you need to keep excellent records to be certain all orders are delivered to the proper people and that none disappear.

Timing is critical. Contact wrapping paper companies by June to set up your holiday program. The company will create a timetable with you. You must get this launched and orders submitted in time to have the wrapping paper back before Thanksgiving. After that, parents panic that it won't arrive in time for the holidays.

VOLUNTEERS

You need someone to chair the committee. Two co-chairs are even better. The chair needs to set up a chain of command. You need volunteers for the following:

- counting out and distributing catalogs
- collecting orders
- tabulating orders and filling out paperwork for the wrapping

paper company

- supervising distribution of orders
- troubleshooting incorrect orders

The number of actual volunteers you need depends upon the size of your school. About five volunteers should be enough for a big school.

A smaller school with 300 students or less can get by with only two volunteers.

SECRETS TO SUCCESS

Deadlines, deadlines! Time yours carefully to get the maximum return in a limited time frame. The best way to handle this is to keep the real set-in-stone deadline to yourself. Give out a first due date that is ten days earlier than the final one. Then give two extensions.

We find about 30 percent of our parents don't hand anything in until the last minute. Giving extensions works best to bring in the maximum number of orders. Set your dates according to the reliability of your parent group.

Put reminders of the deadline for selling wrapping paper in the newsletter. Create flyers for the teachers to insert in the students' backpacks to remind parents to sell wrapping paper and get their orders in on time. Run contests for the most wrapping paper sold per class and offer a pizza or ice cream party for the class with the highest sales.

Have a bar graph in the school lobby charting the progress of each class. Suggest the grandparents also get in on the act and sell to their friends.

HOW MUCH MONEY WILL YOU RAISE?

A big school will raise more money. It's possible that a school of 950 students can net $25,000 or more from a wrapping paper drive. The wrapping paper company should give you an idea how much money a school your size can expect to earn. Even a small school can benefit from this fund-raiser.

TIMELINE

<u>In May of the previous year</u>
Select your wrapping paper company.
<u>By September 20</u>
Distribute catalogs.
<u>3 weeks after distributing catalogs</u>
Process and send in orders.

Before Thanksgiving: Distribute wrapping paper.

JUST STARTING OUT?

This is a good fund-raising event to try if you are just starting out since you don't need to lay out any money in advance.

School Photos

WHAT ARE SCHOOL PHOTOS?

Every elementary school I know takes photos of every school class. The parents association gets almost half the total revenue from these class photos to add to their coffers. Here's a new twist:

- If you have many families whose children graduate to middle schools and high schools that may not have school photos, create a *Family Photo Day* in addition to the regular one.
- More pictures mean more revenue for the school and the photographer.
- Family Photo Day takes place on a Saturday. Anyone can come and get in the picture: Mom, Dad, baby sister, even the dog. There are many families who prefer to have one photo with all their children instead of separate photos for each. This saves money for the family as they only pay for one set of photos instead of one for each child.
- Photo packages can range from $10 to $100. As the price increases, the number of items—photos, magnets, bookmarks—also increases. Family Photo Day helped to generate more income because families that might have turned down photos for three children will pay for this one.

HOW DO FAMILY PHOTOS WORK?

You need to have permission to use the school on Saturday. Ahead of time, email flyers to parents. Put a reminder in your school newsletter. Put up posters around the school. When you have a list of all the families who paid in advance for family photos, set up a schedule.

Allow ten to fifteen minutes between families. Stress to parents they need to be on time.

Word-of-mouth is the best way to find a photographer. Call other schools or parents associations until you find one that is satisfied with their photographer. Reliability and photo quality are more important than having the lowest price. Schedule School Photo and Family Photo Day in the fall so people have them in time for the holidays to enclose with greeting cards or frame as gifts for Grandma and Grandpa.

Unless you have a huge turnout, you should be able to handle family photos in one day. Be sure to have many disposable combs and a mirror on hand.

Photos must be completely paid for in advance because there will be people who change their mind, and the parents association will be stuck paying for those. Schedule a retake day in case some photos turn out badly or get messed up.

VOLUNTEERS

Often the photographer comes with one or two assistants. You may only need two or four volunteers during the day on Family Photo Day to help the photographer's assistants. The photographer should run the show. You may need one or two volunteers to get flyers out to the parents and collect the money before picture day.

SECRETS TO SUCCESS

Family Photo Day extends school photos and increases revenue. Another special feature:

- Make sure every child gets a photo of the whole class, whether they can pay for it or not. The parents association picks up the tab for those few class photos that families can't pay for. Being able to extend a helping hand in this area is one of the many benefits of spending so much time raising money. The families who can't pay really appreciate having class photos for their children.

HOW MUCH MONEY WILL YOU RAISE?

Back in the day our large elementary school raised about $6,000 on school/family photos.

TIMELINE

End of previous school year (May or June)

Select a photographer

- Your photographer will assign a date to your school. Make sure he or she schedules you in time to get the photos back before the holidays. Don't forget to allow for retakes.

JUST STARTING OUT?

This is a good event for you if your school is just starting to raise funds because there is no cash up front required for the photographer.

Pumpkin Sales

WHAT IS A PUMPKIN SALE?

A pumpkin sale takes place when you rent space in the schoolyard to a local farmer to sell his pumpkins. The PA takes charge and keeps the rental money. While this may not earn a lot of money, it's easy to arrange and doesn't require any upfront investment.

HOW DO PUMPKIN SALES WORK?

If you can get permission to use your schoolyard on a Saturday and Sunday, you can invite pumpkin farmers to rent space and sell pumpkins.

- Permission to use school grounds is the first step.
- Research into the nearest pumpkin farmers is the next step.
- Decide how much you want to charge for the space. Find a farmer willing to pay your price and set a date. Or negotiate your terms. After you do this once, you'll have some idea how many pumpkins he can sell. Then you can adjust the space rental rate accordingly. It may be possible to get permission for two weekends, one at the end of September and one the first weekend of October.
- An alternate idea:
  - Don't charge the farmer anything.
  - Have a volunteer handle the pumpkin sales.
  - Split the sales with the farmer. For example, let's say for every ten-dollar pumpkin, five goes to the farmer and five goes to the school. To execute this idea, you'll need some volunteers and a cash box to keep the money.
- You will need a person to handle security during this event. Don't leave a stranger in charge. Also, be sure the seller leaves the space "broom clean."

- Don't go for a deal where the seller gives you a percentage of his take because you won't know exactly how much he's taken in if you don't make the sales.

VOLUNTEERS

This event shouldn't require many volunteers. One to contact a vendor, one to handle security, and two to take the money, if you opt for that way to get paid. Never have one person in charge of the money. Handling cash can prove to be too much temptation for some people. If you have two in charge and of counting the money, you're more likely to avoid internal theft.

SECRETS TO SUCCESS

Timing is crucial to the success of this event. You must have the pumpkins there early enough in September to get sales before they go to grocery stores, but not too early to reap the harvest.

- Find a reliable farmer and use the same one every year. Saves time and heartache.
- Bring paints and brushes and have a pumpkin painting contest on the spot. This will create a buzz and draw attention. Buy three simple —even be large pumpkins—to award at the end of the event.
- Sell pumpkin baked goods at a separate table. Pumpkin muffins and pumpkin pie will also advertise the event and encourage sales of pumpkins.

HOW MUCH MONEY WILL YOU RAISE?

This will vary on the deal you can negotiate with the farmer, how many pumpkins you sell, and what your arrangement is with him. This should be an easy event, and, even if it doesn't make a ton of money, it will put some cash in the PA coffers.

TIMELINE

<u>End of the previous school year (May)</u>

Select a farmer. Secure permission to use the schoolyard.

<u>August</u>

Check back to be sure the crop has not been damaged.

<u>September</u>

Secure volunteers.

<u>Day of the event</u>

Show up early to help set up. Stay to be sure the schoolyard is left "broom clean."

JUST STARTING OUT?

This is a good event to launch your new fund-raising efforts without much work or fuss. No upfront money is necessary.

The Halloween Harvest Festival

WHAT IS A HALLOWEEN HARVEST FESTIVAL?

A Halloween Harvest Festival is like a school fair with food, music, dancing, games, and a haunted house. All the kids and many of the parent volunteers come in costume. The Halloween Harvest Festival can replace traditional Halloween activities. It provides a safe place for our children to celebrate this wacky holiday to the max. Our Halloween Harvest Festival took place in the evening on the Friday closest to, but always before, Halloween and was one of the liveliest, most fun events of the year.

HOW DOES A HALLOWEEN HARVEST FESTIVAL WORK?

Our original Harvest Festival evolved from a small autumn street fair with no real theme. It was a huge amount of work. Enthusiasm waned, we couldn't get volunteers, and the financial return kept shrinking.

We reinvented the Harvest Festival to incorporate Halloween which included these changes: Taking the festival indoors to the gym, hallways, cafeteria, and stairwells from outside in the schoolyard, where the weather was a factor. Adding music and dancing in the gym and a scary Halloween haunted house created in a side stairwell (if you don't have a stairwell, use a room with a door at each end to manage traffic flow).

We added a bake sale, face painting, games in the hallway, and an admission charge, which can include a hotdog, piece of pizza, or soda, too.

Everyone came in costume. It became a huge hit. A successful Halloween Harvest Festival can consist of the following:

- haunted house
- hot dogs, soda, bake sale (see "The Ultimate Bake Sale")

- Hired (or find a volunteer, if you can) DJ with music for dancing in the gym

- free ice cream or soda with $5 admission

- face painting and games in booths or at tables in the hallways next to the gym and cafeteria keep the festivities restricted to specific areas

- grab bags (The grab bags contain inexpensive small Halloween toys and candy bought through catalogs like U.S. Toy and Oriental Trading mixed up in brown paper lunch bags, with no two bags carrying exactly the same items. They cost about 75 cents and sell for $2 each. 150 bags will sell out quickly.)

Put the music in the gym and the games in the hallway just outside. The cafeteria is a good place for the hot dogs, soda, and bake sale.

The best place for the haunted house is a side stairwell. This allows children to enter from one floor and leave from another, avoiding crowding. Also, using the stairwell does not mess up any teacher's classroom. If there are windows in the stairwell, open them to keep the area cool. If you don't have a stairwell—many schools are on one floor—use a classroom or other room with a door at each end. This allows you to have one door as an entrance and one as an exit. Using two doors prevents traffic problems and keeps children moving.

Decorations, except in the haunted house, isn't necessary. Decorating can eat up your budget fast, besides kids and parents in costume come already "decorated". Schedule this event on the Friday before Halloween, unless Halloween is on a Friday. A good start time is 6 p.m., and finish by 9 p.m.

You might price hot dogs and soda a dollar each. A Halloween bake sale brings out the most creative cupcakes I've ever seen. Using icing, candies, sprinkles, and anything else edible, fabulously decorated cupcakes show witches, pumpkins, goblins, or swirling combinations of orange, black and white. Each batch is an example of the wonderful creativity of children brought out by this holiday.

Rock 'n roll music with a DJ and a good boom box adds to the fun. Hire a teenager to take care of the music. After all, what would a Halloween Festival be without dancing to "The Monster Mash" in the gym? Although lighting professionals can create a spectacular spooky house, you don't need them to have a fantastic haunted house. An experienced member of a haunted house team gives this advice:

- Buy lots and lots of black fabric. Use it to cover walls and objects in the room you are using. In the dark, the black fabric gives the illusion that the room is empty. Then you can create your own scary scenes in front of the dark backdrop.
- Dress everyone in black. Buy scary masks or make up the faces of your adult and older child volunteers to be scary creatures like Dracula, ax man, Frankenstein, or other monsters. You're only limited by your own imagination.
- Hold a lit flashlight under your chin to create a creepy look.
- Use lots of props, like fake spiderwebs, a cleaver, and chains.
- Buy a sound-effects tape of eerie noises, like creaking doors.
- For a graveyard effect, create fake tombstones, build a fake coffin, and have someone rise up out of it.

- Make a papier-mâché head using an inflated balloon as the base. Paint it to look ghoulish. Use green olives with pimentos for eyes.
- Use only black lights. They make everything white glow in the dark.
- Hang string to tickle kids' faces in the dark.
- Put stuff on the floor, like bubble wrap that makes noise when stepped on.

- Set up a wire-and-pulley system so you can send a homemade ghost sailing from out of nowhere into the light.
- Paint empty eggshells with Day-Glo paint to make scary eyes.
- Hang up scary critters like skeletons, bats, spiders, ghosts, black cats, and witches that move or have eyes or mouths that move.

- Buy scary rubber hands or stuff rubber gloves.
- Record your own tape with scary laughs, screams, and creaking hinges.

Hang scary things, like glow-in-the-dark skeletons and fake body parts, from the ceiling. Keep it dark to create shadows. Spring out of the darkness to scare the wits out of the children. The big kids get a real kick out of that. Remember that all children, no matter their age, need adult supervision in the haunted house.

Two cautions:

- When younger children come through the haunted house, notify everyone to tone down their performance.
- Use white or glow-in-the-dark tape to tape a trail or guideline on the floor for children to follow.

Save what you buy to use again the following year. That helps keep expenses down, and, in a few years, you'll have a treasure trove of Halloween fright gadgets and supplies.

You can charge $1.00 for each time someone goes through the Haunted House, on top of admission.

Games run the gamut. Face painting is popular, especially for children who don't come in costume. Ring toss, ping-pong ball toss, temporary tattoos, and jewelry making are four examples of the many, many indoor games and activities you can quickly and easily set up at tables. Game booths take more time to create.

Start early. Publicity is very important. In addition to boosting attendance, it can recruit volunteers and get baked good donations, as well. Advertise in your school newsletter. Put up posters in the neighborhood—in local store windows—as well as throughout the school.

With all the concern for children's safety surrounding Halloween, many parents are looking for alternatives to trick or treating for their children. You should attract people beyond your own school.

Security is important. Make sure nothing in the school is damaged. One year, a very concerned parent invested in some wide rolls of plastic. He put the plastic over the artwork on the walls in the halls, insuring it remained unharmed.

Keep children confined to specific parts of the building, with your own security guards—or volunteer parents—to keep people out of off-limits locations. We paid our after-school security staff to handle security for the Halloween Harvest Festival. Negotiate price based on the number of hours they will work.

Remember, security is very important. If the building is trashed or artwork or class work on the walls destroyed, the principal will be reluctant to let you use the school for this event again.

Try these booth ideas:

- Mask Making: Decorate plastic half-masks from the store with glitter, feathers, and stickers. Make your own masks out of cardboard and string or paper bags.

- Milk Carton Crash: Use tennis balls to knock down half-gallon milk cartons (with the tops cut off so they can be stacked.)

- Bean Bag Toss: Toss homemade beanbags into a witch/ghost/Frankenstein's mouth. Make the monster out of sturdy corrugated cardboard. Cut a generous hole for the mouth to make it easier.

- Weird Nails: Use green or black nail polish and nail stickers and glitter to make spooky fingernail designs.

- Cupcake Decorating: This is always popular. Use Halloween-colored icing in orange and black. Add small Halloween candies.
- Pin the Tail on the Donkey: For Halloween, use a Pin the Tail on the Black Cat or Pin the Broom on the Witch. Recruit the best artists in your school to draw the figures.

Collect the admission charge right at the door. This covers the cost of a DJ, music. Then, also at the door, sell tickets for everything else, like hot dogs, haunted house, and games. You can give everyone a free dish of ice cream or soda for the admission price.

Keep access to cash limited to just two or three trustworthy people. I never thought money would disappear in a school, but, sad to say, it does happen. The best way to guard against stealing is by using tickets for everything except admission.

Keep all the cash in one place. Even the bake sale table can use tickets. Our treasurer or assistant treasurer monitors the cash at every event. This consistency provides a safeguard against theft.

VOLUNTEERS

You will need a lot of volunteers to run this event. Start with a chairperson and committee heads. I suggest the following committees:

- food—with two subcommittees: bake sale and hot dog
- music
- haunted house
- games
- publicity
- security
- admissions/tickets.

Each committee chair should be responsible for recruiting his or her own volunteers. But the event chair should help by recruiting and deploying volunteers where they are needed most.

Don't plan to have one person handle a booth alone all evening. Everyone wants to have a good time. Make sure you have enough people helping and taking turns so everyone can dance in the gym and enjoy a hot dog and cupcake.

Older children can be recruited to help in game booths and at the bake sale table, as long as there is an adult there supervising.

SECRETS TO SUCCESS

What really makes this event special is the attitude of everyone involved as well as the haunted house. The parents get excited about this event and that enthusiasm is contagious.

Many other schools and organizations have Halloween parties, but the haunted house takes the party to another level. It is the hit of the evening. The line to get into the haunted house is always long, and children have to be dragged away to go home at closing.

Music is also something unique to this Halloween Harvest Festival. I've been to many Halloween parties and never seen one that included a DJ and dancing in the gym. This provides a safe place for the children to be active and work off some of the sugar they have taken in at the bake sale table.

Our grab bags are unique and best-sellers at every event. I will go into more detail about grab bags in the chapters about the auction and the street fair.

HOW MUCH MONEY WILL YOU RAISE?

Our old original Harvest Festival was producing only $1,500 when we made the changeover. In its first year, the Halloween Harvest Festival produced $5,000. The next year, revenue increased to about $6,200. Although this may not be your biggest moneymaking event, but it sure is a big "fun" raiser.

TIMELINE

<u>End of previous school year (May or June)</u>
Secure date with the school.
Line up chairperson and committee heads, hire DJ.
<u>Early September</u>
Meet with committee chairs to map out locations and plan activities.
<u>End of September</u>
Secure volunteers for each committee.
<u>First week of October</u>
Purchase all grab bag items and decorations.
<u>Week before the event</u>
Stuff grab bags.
<u>Few Days before the event</u>
Purchase food
<u>Day of the event</u>
Create haunted house
JUST STARTING OUT?
This event requires some money up front for haunted house supplies.

- Sell tickets in advance to get some cash for food and supplies.
- Get haunted house supplies donated from local stores.
- Ask parents to contribute or even lend supplies they may have, like old black fabric or Halloween decorations from years past.

- Ask a few parents to purchase supplies and be reimbursed after the event.
- Get the event sponsored by a store or civic organization.
- Because you are charging admission, you will have cash to pay the security guards and the DJ at the end of the evening.

- Skip the hot dogs and just have a bake sale.
- Ask the people doing grab bags to lay out the money for the

small toys in advance and reimburse them when the event is over.

- Have games only at the fair. Games don't usually require much in the way of supplies. For example, knocking down empty milk cartons with a tennis ball is a great game that requires only a few dollars to set up and run.
- Find a teenager or rock 'n roll music buff who is willing to be your DJ for free.

TIP: Oriental Trading may have a special advance purchase Halloween catalog they mail in July. You may get free shipping and save a lot of money by buying your supplies early from this catalog. You can reach them at www.orientaltrading.com[2].

Make sure your publicity is strong. Include posters in key locations in your community, like store windows and pediatricians' offices as well as in school and your newsletter. If you are asking people to lay out money in advance, you need to be sure you will have a big enough turnout to pay them back after the event as well as clear extra revenue for your coffers.

Election Day Bake Sale

(See The Ultimate Bake Sale,)

Don't miss this unique opportunity to raise money from the pockets of those who don't have children in your school.

WINTER EVENTS

Dances

You can create a dance for any reason at any time for any age group. A dance is a classic event that can be put together easily at the last minute. Here are three examples of dances that are easy to run:

SOCK HOP

WHAT IS A SOCK HOP?

A sock hop is a dance with a theme. You play music of your chosen era, 1950's to 1980's, and the kids come dressed in outfits that reflect that time.

COSTUMES

For 1950's the girls wear "poodle skirts," felt circle skirts with a cutout—the poodle was popular—glued on. Poodle skirts are usually done in pastel colors and worn with color-coordinated sweaters and ankle socks. But any version of a skirt and top has a '50s look will do.

A ponytail is the easiest '50s hairstyle, but a pageboy also qualifies. The boys slick their hair back with gel or mousse into the closest version of a DA (duck's ass) as they can get. They roll up the sleeves on short-sleeved shirts or even T-shirts and wear tight pants.

For 1980's, John Travolta's white suit leads the way. Look up the clothing styles of the era you've chosen and suggest clothing ideas to parents and kids in your newsletter.

MUSIC/DANCING

Music from Bill Haley and the Comets, Fats Domino, Elvis, and others is readily available. Parents can teach kids how to do the Lindy or the jitterbug, the most popular dances at that time. You don't really need poodle skirts or ponytails to have a successful sock hop. Just assorted '50s music, some food, and a group of kids ready to dance is enough to have a great event.

Or the music from the movie "Saturday Night Fever" or other popular songs from the 1980's. The Robot, Running Man and even break dancing were popular then.

WHAT DOES A SOCK HOP ENTAIL?

Pick a date for the hop that allows you at least three weeks to complete preparations for the dance with ease. Secure the rights to use your gymnasium on that day. In New York City, we had to pay a custodial fee to keep the building open beyond normal hours. Is that true for your school? Find out before you go ahead with your plans.

Find a DJ. If you hire a professional, you have to pay a fee, which can be expensive. Can you get a few parents together, who have collections of '80s music, or whatever era you want, and ask either a parent or a teenager sibling to be the DJ? You can give a teenager $20 for their time from your proceeds, or just reward them with free pizza, soda, and cupcakes. A parent DJ should do the job as a volunteer and not charge anything.

Not a Sock Hop fan? Try a new dance them, like:

1. Wearing clothes backwards.
2. Coming in pajamas and nightgowns.
3. Western theme with country music.
4. Hawaiian theme with colorful shirts, grass skirts, and fake flower leis.
5. Black-and-white theme. Where everyone dresses only in black and white.
6. Sports theme.
7. Valentine theme.
8. Square Dance.

Food is important. Since we do not have access to the school kitchen when we have a dance, we usually offer a slice of pizza or a can of soda to the parents and kids as part of the price of admission. If you can use the school kitchen, then you can have a potluck or make and sell other food, like hot dogs. Have a bake sale, too.

Put time limits on the dance. Start at 6:30 and throw everyone out at 9:30. For middle or high school kids, you can start later and keep them until 10 or 10:30 p.p. on a Friday or Saturday night.

You must have monitors or chaperones. Hire teachers or get parent volunteers. Pay parents if you have to, but security is mandatory. Restrict the kids to one or two floors or sections of your school at the most and be firm.

Protect the building from rampaging and overactive kids. A few rolls of clear plastic about four of five feet wide can be put on the hall walls to cover and protect artwork.

Without any parental supervision, children can go wild, especially with the sugar from the cupcakes and the provocation of the music. Most kids are fine, but two or three troublemakers can do damage. Even though we told parents they could not just drop their kids off and leave, some did anyway.

Publicity is easy for this event. If you have a school newsletter, put notices in two weeks in advance and again one week in ahead. Hang posters around the school. Hand out fliers at morning school drop-off and at dismissal.

VOLUNTEERS

Dances need fewer parent volunteers than other events. A committee can consist of one person, but two is best.

You need:

1. Small publicity committee
2. Music committee
3. Security committee
4. Decoration committee
5. Food committees: pizza and soda committee and baked goods committee.
6. Someone to check the rules and regulations regarding being in the school at night.
7. Cleanup committee.

SECRETS TO SUCCESS

Charge $5 or $10 at the door for everybody, adult or child. This covers a slice of pizza, soda, and the DJ, if you can't find a parent to do the job. Sell baked goods, at a low price, to keep the evening from being expensive. With a lot of donations of baked goods, you can do quite well. Baked goods can also be thematic, like poodle-decorated cupcakes, polka dots or other '50s images on cookies and cupcakes.

We didn't decorate the gym. Decorations are expensive and the colorful themed clothes do the trick. Middle and high school dances require decoration. Perhaps a committee could get decorations donated by families to avoid adding expenses. Older kids will want to take over decorating for their dances. Or get brightly colored balloons and helium. Float bunches of balloons in special spots.

Form a solid relationship with the local franchise of a pizza chain like Domino's. Domino's supported our local school and scout groups. Domino's gave us pizza at a reduced price because we were a school. That enabled us to clear more money by reducing our expenses.

Don't be afraid to ask for freebies or discounts. A good relationship with your school boosts sales for your local pizza parlor—it's a win/win. In a franchise, speak with the manager. In a mom-and-pop shop, speak with the owner.

Publicize any retail outfit that gives you a break, and encourage families to frequent restaurants and stores that contribute to your school.

Pick up soda at the price club or a beverage warehouse. Get everything as cheaply as possible. Free is even better!

Schedule your dance on a Friday night—the perfect evening for fun family activities before the more heavily scheduled core of the weekend gets going.

HOW MUCH MONEY WILL YOU RAISE?

We made as much as $6,500 on a school dance, although our first dance only made $3,500. It takes a few times to work out the kinks and maximize your profits. That was a while ago. You may raise much more.

TIMELINE

Three weeks ahead

Select a date and okay it with the school.

Three to two weeks ahead

Appoint committee chairs

Decide on food

Hire DJ and security guards

Two weeks ahead:

Start publicity

One week ahead

Negotiate with pizza/soda company

Order food and drinks

Day of the dance

Put up plastic protection on walls,

Post Stop signs to keep kids in designated areas

VALENTINE'S DAY DANCE

This theme offers almost limitless ideas for cupcake and gym decorations. It also allows for a broader range of music. A Valentine's Day Dance in the dead of winter can really pick up everybody's spirits.

SQUARE DANCE

This dance theme, which lends itself to a country-and-western motif in both baked goods (do you know how to make a shoofly or sweet potato pie?), clothing, and gym decoration. One benefit of a square dance is that the caller tells everybody what to do, so kids who might be shy or don't know how to dance can join in instantly.

Also, as with a circle dance, square dancing sometimes doesn't require a specific partner. Even if you do have a partner, it isn't an intimate slow dance. One drawback is that you must hire a caller, which can be expensive and possibly hard to find in your area. Maybe a parent in your school would volunteer to be the caller? Advertise the need for this position in your school newsletter. The square dance was our first successful dance at P.S. 87.

Other possible dance themes might include: St. Patrick's Day, May Day, Sadie Hawkins (girls ask the boys—for older children), Folk Dance, First Day of Spring, or any special occasion happening in your school.

JUST STARTING OUT?

You can have a dance without all the expense by:

- Having potluck food instead of hot dogs and pizza.
- Use a volunteer DJ.
- Get a corporate sponsor. Maybe the senior class would like to sponsor the dance, which means that parents of the seniors would chip in and pay the expenses.

- Don't get anything you have to pay for in advance. Pay the DJ, pizza, and soda out of proceeds at the door. This can be risky—if you don't make enough at the door, someone will have to foot the bill.

Friday Night Pizza And A Movie

WHAT IS FRIDAY NIGHT PIZZA AND A MOVIE?

` Friday Night Pizza and a Movie at school was invented to combat the winter blahs and answer the eternal Friday night question, "What are we doing tonight?"

WHAT DOES FRIDAY NIGHT PIZZA AND A MOVIE INVOLVE?

On Friday nights in January, February, and March, the PA serves pizza at 6:30 p.m. and show a kids' movie in the school auditorium at 7:00. Schedule an intermission in the middle of the movie for a bathroom break and to sell popcorn, soda, and chocolate milk for $1 each. Adding a baked goods table will raise revenue. Wind the evening up around nine, depending upon the length of the movie.

You don't have to use current movies. You might consider showing classics like *Spaceballs* and *The Wizard of Oz*. You can't rent movies to show because of the legal restrictions of showing a rented movie for profit. But you can use movies you own. Comb the parent body for video suggestions. You can use a big screen TV and a DVD player, or projector and screen.

You can charge $10 per person. This includes pizza, a drink, the movie, security, and the cost of renting the school, if you have to pay. You might not make much money, but this event is a community builder. Over time, the small profit will add up.

In the meantime, the parents and kids have a wonderful time being together. Negotiate with a local pizza parlor for a low price since you will be ordering weekly for three months.

VOLUNTEERS

This event doesn't require many volunteers, but you do need people each week. It's a good idea to have at least one board member there each week to oversee the event. You'll need a food committee, a movie committee, security/building committee to be certain security people are present and that you have permission to use the building every week, and a clean-up committee. One person can handle publicity. There will be plenty of word-of-mouth advertising, too. Post the upcoming movies in your school newsletter and place a few posters reminding people which movie is playing each week.

SECRETS OF SUCCESS

We screened our first movie for sixty people. That was quite the turnout. We allowed parents of children in third grade and up to just drop their children off and leave. This became a wonderful way for the parents to let the kids have an independent experience safely. It gave parents the opportunity to run out to dinner without paying a sitter.

Can you afford a long square carnival-style popcorn machine? It will make professional popcorn you can sell cheaply. No funds for that right now? Use a microwave and microwave popcorn instead.

Here is a list of older, classic movies that would be appropriate to show:

Homeward Bound (both 1 and 2)
Beethoven (1 through 4)
Andre
Free Willy (1 and 2)
Air Bud
Dustan Checks In
Dr. Doolittle (1 and 2)
Spy Kids
The Incredible Journey
That Darn Cat (2 only)
I'll Fly Away
Milo & Otis
The Goonies
The Santa Clause
Jingle All the Way
Miracle on 34th Street (the original only)

Snow Day
Alaska
Sandlot
The Princess Diaries
Anything Disney

HOW MUCH MONEY WILL YOU RAISE?

After two and a half months, we raised almost $4,000 dollars. Your profit depends upon how much you can charge, how high attendance is, and how cheaply you can buy pizza. Some movies will pull more people than others. It takes time to discover which movies work best. After a month or so, you'll know more what kind of movies to show. But this is more about building community and providing a service than it is about raising a ton of money.

TIMELINE

This event does not need much advance preparation.

<u>Beginning of the school year, or as soon as possible</u>

Secure the right to use the school.

<u>In December</u>

Select the first three movies.

Start Publicity

<u>End of December</u>

Negotiate with Pizza Parlor

More movies can be selected during the first three weeks. Publicity should be ongoing.

Holiday Shopping Day For Kids

WHAT IS A HOLIDAY SHOPPING DAY FOR KIDS?

This is a Saturday event where the school is open only to children shopping for Christmas or Hanukkah gifts for their families. The parents buy, make, or donate items that would make appropriate gifts. The children come to school with a few dollars in their pockets and buy whatever they feel they want to give as gifts. The items must be priced reasonably so the children don't have to spend too much money. The money used to buy the gifts goes to the PA.

HOW DOES KIDS' SHOPPING DAY WORK?

You need parents in your school to make and donate lots of things or who are willing to buy and donate items to make this fund-raiser work. Try a gift-wrapping table. For a dollar, you can wrap each gift. This works if someone donates wrapping paper.

First, find donors. When you think you have enough, select a day and start publicity.

VOLUNTEERS

You will need parents to shepherd the children through the sale and parents to make change and wrap gifts. As always, have parents on hand to handle security. The number of volunteers you need depends upon the size of the sale and the number of children buying.

HOW MUCH MONEY WILL YOU RAISE?

This event can raise anywhere from $100 to $1,000, depending upon the size of your school and the size of your sale. This is not so much a fund-raiser as it is a fun day and a service for kids, teaching them the joy of giving.

TIMELINE

<u>Two months ahead</u>

Line up donors and volunteers

<u>One month ahead</u>

Start publicity, get wrapping paper.

<u>Day before</u>

Organize sale items.

Set up displays on tables in the gym or cafeteria.

<u>Day of</u>

Get security set up.

Have volunteers in the room with the children to help.

Christmas Tree Sales

WHAT IS A CHRISTMAS TREE SALE?

A Christmas tree sale takes place when you rent space in the schoolyard to a local Christmas tree farmer to sell his trees. The PA keeps the rental money. While this may not earn a lot, it's easy to arrange and doesn't require any upfront investment.

TIP: Set up tables outside and rent them to parents or others to sell their craft items or to authors to sell their books for the holidays. Publicize it in the newsletter. You might draw more people than a Christmas tree sale alone, benefitting both the farmer and the PA.

HOW DO CHRISTMAS TREE SALES WORK?

If you can get permission to use your schoolyard on a Saturday and Sunday, you can invite tree farmers to rent space.

- Permission to use school grounds is the first step.
- Research into the nearest Christmas tree supplier is the next step.
- Decide how much you want to charge for the space. Find a tree grower willing to pay your price and set a date. If you can't find someone to pay your asking price, lower it. Best to have some money coming in than nothing. This doesn't cost the PA a dime, so some revenue is better than none.
- After the first time, you'll have an idea how many trees can be sold. You can adjust the rent according to the volume of trees, too.
- It may be possible to get permission for two weekends—one right after Thanksgiving and the other the following week.
- You'll need a person to handle security. Don't leave a stranger in charge. Also, be sure the seller leaves the schoolyard "broom clean."
- Don't go for a deal where the seller gives you a percentage of

his take because you won't know exactly how much he's taken in if you don't make the sales yourself. A set fee when your start out is reliable.

VOLUNTEERS

This event shouldn't require many volunteers. One to contact a vendor, one to handle security, and two to take the money. Never have one person in charge of the money. Handling cash can prove to be too much temptation for some people. If you have two in charge of and counting the money, you're more likely to avoid internal theft.

SECRETS TO SUCCESS

Timing is crucial to the success of this event. You must have the trees there at the best time. When do people buy their holiday trees in your town? Be sure not to do this too late in the month, or it will flop.

- Find a reliable farmer and use the same one every year. Saves time and headache.
- Buy the makings of Christmas ornaments and decorations. Set crafts up at separate tables and charge a modest fee.
- Sell Christmas cookies and other holiday-themed baked goods at a separate table.

HOW MUCH MONEY WILL YOU RAISE?

This will vary on the deal you can negotiate with the farmer, how many Christmas trees you sell, and what your arrangement is with him. This should be an easy event, and even if it doesn't make a ton of money, it will put some cash in the PA coffers.

TIMELINE

<u>End of the previous school year (May)</u>

Select a farmer. Secure permission to use the yard.

<u>August</u>

Check back to be sure the crop has not been damaged.

<u>September</u>

Secure volunteers.

<u>Day of the event</u>

Show up early to help set up. Stay to be sure the schoolyard is left "broom clean."

JUST STARTING OUT?

This is a good event to launch your new fund-raising efforts without much work or fuss. No upfront money is necessary.

Family Game Night

WHAT IS FAMILY GAME NIGHT?

Family game night is an event where families bring games to school and play with their children.

HOW DOES FAMILY GAME NIGHT WORK?

Families bring their favorite games. From board games, like Life, Clue, or Checkers, to more interactive games, like Charades, and the gym or cafeteria is filled with games and parents and kids. If you use the gym, you'll need tables and chairs, but probably not in the cafeteria.

Games are set up on tables, and people sit down to play. When a game is finished, the players move on to another game. It's best to pick shorter games, like Sorry, rather than *Monopoly*, which can take a long time. Dominoes, checkers, chess, and backgammon are great games to add to the mix.

If you're playing games in the gym, start the evening early by having a potluck in the cafeteria. Add a bake sale to raise money.

Consider charging per family. Perhaps ten or twenty dollars plus one dish per family to eat and play. Furnish drinks free. Start the evening at six and finish up at nine.

VOLUNTEERS

You'll need volunteers to run the potluck and keep things moving at the game tables. You'll also need someone to make a list of which family brought which game, so they can be returned to their owners at the end of the evening.

Two people are needed to handle money. And at least one person in charge of security, though two are better, since you may be using two rooms.

One person should be able to handle publicity.

SECRETS TO SUCCESS

This event can be run more than once a year. It should be perfect for winter bad weather days, when it's cold outside, and when everyone has cabin fever. You probably need to run this event several times to figure out which games are the most popular.

Weed out the unpopular ones and advertise the ones that are the biggest draw. If a game is super popular, set it up on several tables. If that means that the PA buys games for game night, okay. It would be a good use of some of the money.

If possible, have game night once in the fall, in the winter, and spring.

HOW MUCH MONEY WILL YOU RAISE?

This is an event that may take time and good word-of-mouth to build in popularity. Your first night, you may only make a little money. If you have ten families, that's $100!

But as kids and parents talk about the fun they had, other families will come out for the second game night. Don't get discouraged if you don't break the bank on the first one.

TIMELINE

<u>September</u>

Plan which 1, 2 or 3 nights you'll have game night.

Get permission from the school. Start publicity.

<u>A week before</u>

Remind custodians that you'll need tables and chairs in the gym. Run publicity in your newsletter and put up posters.

<u>Night of the event</u>

Arrive early to make sure everything is set up.

JUST STARTING OUT?

This is perfect for just starting out as it doesn't require any money up front.

In-School Garage Sale

WHAT IS AN IN-SCHOOL GARAGE SALE?

It is a sale of secondhand merchandise held inside the school. Parents, teachers, and staff lug their treasures they no longer prize to the school to sell for a low price to others.

HOW DOES AN IN-SCHOOL GARAGE SALE WORK?

Organize one to take place inside your school in the winter. Give parents teachers and school staff an opportunity to get rid of stuff they no longer want and maybe make a few bucks to boot.

Set up tables in the gym. If your school doesn't own large folding tables, the PA should buy them with funds raised. They will pay for themselves in no time.

Charge $25 or more per table. Run the sale on a Saturday. Get the kids involved. It's a perfect opportunity for the simple math lesson of making change.

Make it clear to participants they must cart away any unsold items themselves. The PA cannot be responsible for things left in the gym. Slip a generous tip to the custodians to be there and cart away trash.

Publicity: use your newsletter to recruit participants and to advertise the event. Put up posters in the school.

Publish your guidelines, too. I'd recommend not allowing books. Secondhand books could be a sale in itself (See Book Exchange). But when mixed with other items, books tend to clog tables. You might want to restrict the sale of furniture, especially beds. Stress that any clothing sold must be in good condition and recently washed or dry cleaned.

Sellers must be responsible for collecting their own money and making change.

TIP: *Repeat this in the warmer weather outside, in the schoolyard.*
VOLUNTEERS

You will need the following volunteers: Banking (two people to collect and count the money), two parents for security, one organizer who assigns the tables and creates a chart, one parent to troubleshoot, and several parents to organize and run a bake/pizza sale.

SECRETS TO SUCCESS

Beef up what you earn by running a bake sale at the same time. Include coffee and drinks, as well. Pizzas bought by the pie and sold by the slice will raise more money for the PA and keep hungry buyers and sellers happy.

Notify the local media, place posters in store windows (with the store's permission), and on street lamps and public bulletin boards to attract local residents to the sale.

HOW MUCH MONEY WILL YOU RAISE?

If you can fit twenty tables in the gym, you'll make $500 right off the bat. Additional money from the bake/pizza and drinks sale can't be estimated.

TIMELINE

September
Pick a date and get the okay from the principal to use that day.
Eight weeks ahead
Post the date and time in the newsletter and in posters.
Send press releases to local media to bring buyers.
One week ahead
Compile a list of sellers and their table numbers.
Draw a map of the room and number each table.
Email to the participants. Remind bake sale donors.
Day before
Order pizza, pick up soda, juice, and ice.

JUST STARTING OUT?

This is another event that's good for a PA without funds—unless you need to buy tables. If you have tables, there is no dollar outlay required for this event. It's pure profit and a great place to start.

Wine Tasting

WHAT IS A WINE TASTING?

A wine tasting is when a company that sells wine offers prospective buyers the opportunity to sample their wines. Often, tasters who find wines they like buy them. This is a sales tool for the wine company that can be turned into a money-making event for the PA.

HOW DOES A WINE TASTING WORK?

First, you need to connect with a wine or liquor store that carries wine. Talk with the store manager and listen to their suggestions. You may need permission from the school to have alcohol there, even if it's on a Saturday night.

If that doesn't work, you can hold the event either at someone's home or at the store itself, if it's large enough or has a backyard.

The PA would sell tickets at maybe $20 a couple or simply $15 per person—whatever you think will work with your parents.

With money you have in reserve, buy some popular cheeses and crackers to offer along with the wine.

The store will make money from the bottles it sells, so all of the ticket-price revenue should come to the PA.

TIP: Connect with a local winery and hold the event at their location. Charge admission and let the winery charge for bottles and full glasses sold. Saves much work for your parents and makes the event festive. Avoids the issue of serving alcohol in the school.

VOLUNTEERS

This is one of the easier events with few volunteers needed. Of course, you'll need the

treasurer and assistant treasurer to take the money and dispense tickets. You'll need security and a clean-up committee if it's in the school. A publicity committee is vital.

SECRETS TO SUCCESS

An event for children at the school (like a movie) while the wine tasting is somewhere else, can provide childcare, allowing the parents to go to the wine tasting for a few hours without needing a babysitter. Or schedule the wine tasting on a Friday Night Pizza and a Movie night for the kids. Providing a child-friendly event may increase attendance at the wine tasting.

If the PA has money, they should buy a couple of bottles of wine to raffle off at the tasting. If local laws allow you to sell raffle tickets, do so. If not, give out the raffle tickets free. The prospect of winning something can spike attendance.

HOW MUCH MONEY WILL YOU RAISE?

Your profits will depend on your parent body—how much they like wine—and how well you do publicity. If you sell 100 tickets at $15, you'll raise $1,500. But even sales of only 30 tickets will bring you a profit of $450.

If this event is well received, you can count on more participation the next year as word-of-mouth is the best advertising.

TIMELINE

September

Connect with a wine or liquor store and fix a date for the tasting. Recruit volunteers.

Six weeks ahead

Begin publicity.

Start admission ticket and raffle ticket sales.

Two weeks ahead

Do reminder publicity. Check with the wine or liquor store.

Day before

Buy cheese and crackers and drop them off at the store. If you're having the event in school, either store the cheese in a refrigerator there or have a volunteer store then bring to the event.

JUST STARTING OUT?

This is an event that can be done without upfront money. You don't have to have cheese, or you can buy cheese from the proceeds from ticket sales. The same is true for a wine raffle basket. From the proceeds from ticket sales, buy wine from the store, hopefully at a discount, to raffle off.

The Auction

The auction is one of the biggest events of the year. Think of it as the party for parents—no children allowed. It takes place in the evening, and most people dress up. At the auction, many items and services are sold, much wine is drunk, delicious food is eaten, and a *huge* amount of money is raised.

WHAT IS AN AUCTION?

An auction is a gathering where people bid against each other for donated goods and services. Two types of auctions take place during the evening: live and silent. The live auction is where one person stands up and auctions things off one at a time and people in the audience raise their hand or numbered paddle to signal their bids for the items.

A silent auction is where the actual item being auctioned off—or a description of the item printed on a piece of paper—is available for viewing and people write down their names and their bids for the item on the paper.

The items always go to the highest bidder. People must pay that evening for items they have won at the auction. Payment is usually made by cash, check, or credit card. To accept credit cards, you need a merchant account from a bank, which you can get if you are a not-for-profit or a 501c3 nonprofit corporation. Get MasterCard and Visa merchant accounts through the bank where your parents association does business. The bank can instruct you how to fill out all the necessary forms. You should receive a check from the credit card company—MasterCard and VISA for example—directly.

Adding the credit card option makes your auction more successful by allowing people to bid higher, even if they don't have the cash at that moment. And checkout will move faster.

HOW DOES AN AUCTION WORK?

Running an auction is a big project. Here are a few steps you need to get started:

- Put together your auction committee with these committee heads:
  - Space (are you using the school or will you be renting space for the event?)
  - Food (you'll need a caterer unless you have a potluck along with your auction.)
  - Publicity
  - Silent auction
  - Live auction (select parents who are comfortable in front of an audience to be your auctioneers)

- Decorations
- Grab bag
- Local canvassers
- Bazaar table
- Setup
- Catalog
- Cleanup
- Raffle
- Banking
- Tickets

- It is best to have auction co-chairs running the event because there is too much work for one person. It's good to have enough volunteers to have co-chairs for each committee.
- Set the date for the auction early. My school auctions took place on a Saturday night in March, when there are no school vacations and no other big fund-raising events to get in the way. Inform the parent population right away of the date you

select so they can put it on their calendar.

- Have donation forms printed up in triplicate with different colors for each sheet. You need one copy for the donor (yellow), one copy for the winner (white), and one copy for the auction committee to keep records (pink).

- Find a location for you auction. We started out in a school, but the auction grew fast. We moved it to the New York Historical Society, but that venue became too small, too. We ended up in a cavernous church giving us the space we needed for each part of the auction, food, chairs, a bar, and decorations.

- As you would for any special event, book the room well in advance. This requires an estimate of the number of attendees at your auction. Our peak year we had over 600 people, but we had a big school of 950 kids. You'll need to put down a deposit to hold the date for your space, if it's not at your school. See the "Just Starting Out" section that follows to avoid this expense.

- Find a caterer who will do a light, attractive meal or grazing with finger foods for a low rate. Maybe you can find one among your school parents who would do it for cost? Ticket prices should cover the food, if possible. Most years, the tickets just broke even on the cost of the meal. Our tickets grew to be $20 per person. But $15 or less is better if you can do it and not lose money.

If you raise the price, give away a glass of wine with each ticket, if possible. It is essential to get the wine donated; then you can sell it for $5 per additional glass and make money. A high price for wine will make it too expensive. You want to be sure the attendees have plenty of money to spend on auction items.

- Create a theme. Honoring a principal or other long-time staff member gives makes the event about more than simply making money. Sometimes, the honoree lends an idea for a theme. For example, if you honored a teacher, you can use the theme of artist's palettes and paintbrushes for invitations. Honoring a local political figure who has done things for your school is a good way of saying "thank you." You may boost attendance because your politician's friends, relatives, and political connections might attend, too.

- Consider any of these auction themes:

- Black-and-White Ball
- Honoring art in the school
- Honoring a district leader: the mayor, principal, teachers, local political figure
- Spring theme with lots of fresh and paper flowers
- Country western theme
- Mystery theme
- Honoring great parent volunteer, PA president, outstanding custodian, gym or music teacher
- Author's night: invite authors; theme is books and reading
- Dedicated to raising money for the library, science lab, computer lab
- Elegant dessert and champagne dress-up
- Beach motif/Hawaiian night
- Midnight in Paris
- Sunny Spain or Mexican night with appropriate music and food
- Art Gallery: using kids' art
- Safari/Wild Animal/Jungle theme
- Bird watchers or just birds theme
- Dogs or Cats or both
- Alpine Theme

- Give free tickets to your teachers. It is a nice payback for all the wonderful things your teachers do all year long for your children. Don't be upset if teachers don't show up. Saturday night is family time for them. Some may fear parents will corner them and complain, whine, or ask about their children.

• Create attractive invitations. Send them home in the children's backpacks to avoid the cost of postage. Or email invitations. Use snail mail for the folks without email.

LIVE AUCTION

This is the biggest event of the evening. The live auction comes after everything else is completed, including dinner. You can hold the attention of your audience through about 34 items or packages. Too many more and you lose people's attention. The items in a live auction are the biggest, most sought after, most expensive items you have. All the live auction items are written up in detail in your auction catalog.

Sometimes, live auction items are solo—a pair of courtside tickets to a Knicks game, for example—and sometimes they are grouped together, like theater tickets, dinner for two, and a limousine in one package. The auction team creates packages by sorting through all the donations and putting things together.

For example, if someone donates the gym at a local church then a birthday party package would be created to include: the gym, a donation of cupcakes from one family, goodie bags from another, and two hours of basketball instruction for two teams from the gym teacher. Voila—a basketball birthday party package for the live auction. While those items separately might not generate high bids, a complete basketball birthday party could go for several hundred dollars.

When we get an airfare donation and a swanky hotel or condominium donation, we create dream vacation packages. A package like that can go for $2,000 to $3,000 or more.

Other packages might include tickets to the symphony, babysitting services, dinner, and a limousine, or tickets to a sporting event plus a signed hockey stick and baseball cap. Making up packages for the live auction is fun.

SILENT AUCTION

This is where you put your items and services that cannot be used or packaged for the live auction. Often, they command a lower price than live auction items. You can use a large number of silent auction items, many more than in the live auction, as people gravitate to the type of items they are interested in. The more items, the better you'll do. Even if the silent auction items go for less money, it is all pure profit for the school. Divide your donations into categories, such as:

1. Tickets—concerts, plays, sporting events.

1. Class projects—This category was invented by our terrific teachers. Our class projects include lots of creative ideas, like decorated shower curtains or sheets or pillowcases or murals, gift baskets of items donated by parents of a particular class or bought with funds raised from a bake sale.

1. Educational—Any courses you can get donated from any educational institution are good. Classes in pottery or creative writing work, too.

1. Services (Consulting) —Request donations of: wills from lawyers; computer installation; lessons on Microsoft Word, Excel or PowerPoint, room painting; furniture assembly; bookcase built to order; dog walking; babysitting; ironing; extermination; errand running; chiropractic exam; massage; manicure; pedicure; three hours with a professional organizer; estate planning; ninety minutes of computer troubleshooting; tax preparation; home decorating; architect walk-through and advice; graphic design of letterhead, business card, and envelope; the list is endless.

1. Day camps/camps—Approach a day camp or sleep-away camp for either a free week, month, or a discounted price.

1. Lessons—Almost any parent in your school can offer some sort of lesson. Here are a few examples: cooking, baking, computer software, piano or other musical instrument, skiing, ice skating, dance, painting, ceramics, photography, singing, speech and language screening for adult or child, drama coaching, swimming lessons, tennis lessons, soccer coaching, basketball coaching, baseball coaching, origami, calligraphy, knitting, crocheting, sewing, and so on.

A free lesson might inspire someone to hire your donor or pay for their service. Use that idea to sell your parents on donating lessons.

1. Equipment—computers and extra equipment, photography equipment, new tools, art supplies, small kitchen appliances. Everything must be brand-new. Save used items for the white elephant sale at your street fair.

1. Books—This category is tricky. If you have single books, put them on the bazaar table. But collections of books, like the four craft books donated by my publisher friend do better as a set. One year, I also got four cookbooks by the same publisher. We put these two sets in the silent auction and sold them as sets. Instead of getting $5 per book, which is what we would have gotten at the bazaar table, we got $80 for each set of four books, and the bidding was hot and heavy.

1. Jewelry, clothing, and

accessories—Get jewelry donations from local shops and from parents in your school who make jewelry. Get handmade knit and crocheted clothing. We always have the most original jewelry made by parents, and the bidding is good for these one-of-a-kind pieces.

1. Tutoring—This category is like the

lesson category but more specifically for students and academic subjects. Teachers and expert parents offer tutoring on all subjects from science to Spanish and especially that new math that seems to trip up parents. People bid high for tutoring to help their children.

1. Music—This category is similar to

the book category in that bigger bids are generated if your donations are packaged. A parent in the music business, donated a collection of fifty CDs by various groups. That collection sold well. A music business colleague of mine donated hard-to-find collections, like Beethoven's sonatas, which sold for $80.

1. Software—Offer everything from

business software to computer games. We had incredibly competitive bidding for the *Mad Magazine* complete collection on CD-ROM. Although it was selling on the Internet for $49.96, it sold in our auction for over $100.

1. Memberships—Country clubs, gyms, golf courses and anything else that requires a fee to get in. Most of our local gyms offer free one-week trail memberships. A country club might offer something off on their initiation fee or free use of the pool for two weeks.

1. Artwork—This is a broad category. We have sold fabulous paintings by talented artists who are parents in our school.

Several of these went for over $1,000. One year one of our artists made masks of several different people, painted them in exotic colors and attached whimsical ribbons on them. They were beautiful and sold out quickly. Anything interesting, unusual, or original can be sold. Look around. You probably have artists in your parent body that you don't even know about.

1. Uniquely your school—lunch with, breakfast with, museum visit with, at the movies with any classroom teacher, librarian, music teacher, gym teacher, or assistant principal. A great item that we put in our live auction because it does so well is Principal for a Day. You can expand that to include assistant principal, librarian, gym teacher, music teacher for a day, if you have cooperative staff. Buy or wrangle of a donation of unfinished furniture and have a well-known artist or your child's class paint or decorate it and auction it off.

1. Health & Beauty—acupuncture, haircuts galore, free exam & pair of eyeglasses, bike rentals, beauty makeover, day at spa, hair cornrowing, free exam at vet clinic, messenger package service, five hundred copies at a copy shop, free cell phone with one-year contract, quilts and afghans, pet shop gift certificate, moving company gift certificate.

1. Memorabilia—Vintage photos of famous people, collectible dolls, autographed soccer ball, basketball, baseball, even autographs of famous people.

1. Special parties—custom cake to feed fifty, jewelry-making party, gingerbread house-making party, church space rental, gym rental, dinner with famous author (or other person) or the mayor, origami party. Tickets—-Tickets to rehearsals

(ballet, soap opera, play), Disney World, Universal Studios, taping of a TV Show, sporting events, local theater, even movies (ten tickets feels substantial)

1. Miscellaneous—Firehouse tour, radio or TV station tour, tour of sports stadium. Stores that are closing might be good places to hit up for donations. One carpet store in our neighborhood that was moving donated a beautiful oriental carpet that went for $800 in our live auction.

- If you seek donations from chain

stores like Home Depot or Talbot's, you have to go to their national/corporate headquarters. This takes a long time, so plan ahead. Some chain stores make their donations a year in advance, so be sure to get your school's name on their list for next year.

- Make sure all items are legitimate

and there are no strings attached. For example, we wanted to sell a sleepover birthday party in the gym. This would have been a great item and would have generated terrific competitive bidding. But the Board of Education said we couldn't do it. Check it out before accepting an item.

- Create item certificates from the Auction Contract donors have filled out. Certificates look official and provide the information needed for the winner to get in touch with the donor to receive the item or service purchased. You can get nice certificate paper from Staples or Paper Direct on the Internet at www.paperdirect.com[1] Or use the certificate template in Word and print it out on regular paper.

- Bring extra blank certificate sheets for on-the-spot donations that are too small for the live auction.

TIP: *Start the silent auction online or designate some items to be auctioned off online, instead of at the event. Creates buzz and excitement for the event.*

BAZAAR TABLE

The bazaar table is a place to put all the items that cannot become part of a live auction package and won't sustain enough bidding or command a high enough price to go into the silent auction. This is the table with low-price items. Some examples of bazaar table items are: new housewares; single books (preferably hardback); accessories like matching scarf, hat and gloves; new baby clothes; new knickknacks; new videos; single CDs; or software.

MYSTERY CERTIFICATES

Gift certificates to be sold individually like dinner for two or $15.00 worth of dry cleaning are a big hit. You know the value of what you bought will be higher than what you're paying. Attach them to mystery books. For an art theme, tape the certificates to cardboard artist palettes you made. Divide these up into mystery certificates that sell for: $10, $20, $30, $40, and $50. That depends upon what your donations are.

Each mystery certificate should sell for at least $10 less than the value of the certificate being sold. If you have any $5 or $10 gift certificates or items, put them together. If the buyer doesn't get a good value, he or she will be unhappy. Why pay $20 for a $20 gift certificate?

Here are a few samples of the type of items in this category:

- a bottle of wine of your choice from the local liquor store

---

1.   http://www.paperdirect.com

- shoe repair gift certificate
- gift certificate to florist or nursery
- five or ten free video rentals from video store
- haircut for kids
- gift certificate for dry cleaning
- deli gift certificate
- hardware store gift certificate
- music/book store gift certificate
- candy store gift certificate
- lunch at local restaurant
- brunch at local restaurant
- dinner at low-price local restaurant
- pet shop gift certificate
- pizzeria—-one pie gift certificate
- pharmacy gift certificate
- toy store gift certificate
- supermarket gift certificate
- art gallery gift certificate
- bakery gift certificate
- take-out food gift certificate
- fish market gift certificate
- paint store gift certificate
- three-month gym membership
- museum guest passes
- personal trainer
- dinner at your home
- one-year subscription to a magazine

Parents can donate many of these items. A parent who doesn't know what to donate can buy a gift certificate to any store or shop and donate that or buy a magazine subscription to donate. The Mystery

Certificates are popular because everyone knows they will get a great value, and often, these are the first things sold out at the auction.

GRAB BAGS

I think of children when I think of grab bags (see "The Street Fair"). The idea for these auction grab bags for women was a happy accident. I was having breakfast with a friend the year she was auction chair to discuss her new ideas.

She suggested giving away bags of promotional things, like free certificates and product samples from companies sponsoring the auction, to all attendees. A great idea and a good way to promote sponsorship. She considered selling space in the promotional bags for companies not sponsoring the auction to distribute product samples and discount coupons to hawk their merchandise.

I had been in charge of grab bags for kids at the street fair for the previous five years. Those grab bags were filled with donations of all sorts of promotional items, from key chains with bank logos to ballcaps from various companies.

Even though I heard promotional bags, I mistakenly thought she meant grab bags. It was then that we got the idea of selling women's grab bags filled with promotional goodies and samples for women.

We were lucky enough to have several parents connected to cosmetics companies in our parents association. We got fabulous donations from Avon, Estee Lauder, and Yves St. Laurent.

We put together terrific bags containing lipstick, powder, lotions, eye makeup, jewelry, perfume, nail polish, and other small items. We sold them for $5 each. The first year, these bags sold slowly as they were new and no one really knew what to expect.

They were packaged in brown paper lunch bags, so no one knew what was inside. But that did not make them very attractive. Even the fabulous Yves St. Laurent perfume samples in the most exquisite package ever only promoted people to buy a 150 of the 300 bags we'd made.

The second year we only made 150 bags. They sold better, but it was hard to get rid of the last fifteen or so. The third year, we made 150 bags but packaged them in beautiful small Avon blue-and-white shopping bags, and they flew off the table. We had people so disappointed the bags had sold out we increased the number to 200 bags the next year. They sold in an hour. Here is what we put in our grab bags for women:

- lipsticks
- nail polish
- eyeliner pencils
- mascara
- rings, bracelets, necklaces, earrings
- fake flowers,
- discount coupons for photo finishing
- compacts
- watches
- makeup bags
- cream of all sorts
- scents and perfumes
- bubble bath or shower gel samples

Remaindered cosmetics and perfumes are great. Or go back to Jane's original idea and turn the grab bags into promotional bags for local or national merchants to use to distribute discount or free trial coupons and free product samples. Stores and manufacturers might even pay a promotional fee to have samples distributed to the parents in your school.

For our cosmetics grab bags, we charge $5, a great bargain. For strictly promotional bags, you probably can't charge as much. But spending $2 for a bag full of free opportunities at local merchants may be the right way to use grab bags for your school.

If you can't get nice small shopping bags at the local discount store, you can purchase them from Oriental Trading. Go to their Web site: www.orientaltrading.com[2] to order the bags directly or to order a catalog and place your order by phone. Grab bags make great Mother's Day gifts.

2.   http://www.orientaltrading.com

50/50 RAFFLE

This is a very special raffle that we don't use at any other function. Unlike a usual raffle, it involves no prizes at all. Instead, money is the prize. A 50/50 raffle ticket offers a chance to win half of the money collected from the sale of the tickets. If you sell $1,000 worth of tickets, the winner collects $500. This is especially effective at the auction because most of the time the winner turns around and spends the $500 in cash on auction items.

This is a very easy raffle to conduct since tickets are only sold at the auction and there are no prizes involved. All you need are the tickets and good publicity. Announce the raffle several times over a loudspeaker or microphone during the auction.

SETTING UP THE BIDDING

Assigning opening bids:

1. Make them low enough to get things started.

1. An opening bid is not the value of the item. Explain that to donors, who worry that a low opening bid is a negative comment about their donation. If people want something, they will bid high for it. One of the staff members at Job Path offered her services as a personal trainer. (Job Path is a nonprofit organization that finds jobs for people with developmental disabilities.) We put the item in the silent auction and started the bidding at $25, not certain if people would want this or not, and we wanted to make it easy to get the bidding started. The session went for $185!

1. Making low opening bids serves another function. If you have an item you are not sure will sell, and it's a product made by a parent or service donated by a parent or teacher and you are concerned the donor will be upset and hurt if no one bids on the item, a low opening bid allows a friend to bid on it or for

the auction committee to put in a starting bid, using money generated by the auction to win the item.

This is so important. People's feelings can be seriously hurt or they can feel a sense of public humiliation if their special blanket, picture, or offer of advice is left on the table with no one bidding on it. Be sure to have a plan to bail out these generous folks and you will always have donors. Even if you buy the item or service, you don't have to use it. But your donor will feel he or she did their part.

1. Bidding increments for silent auction items should be $5, $10, $15, or $25. For the live auction, bidding increments of $25, $50 or even $60 should be used. Give the auctioneer leeway to do whatever he or she feels is right for the moment. Sometimes, if an item is hot, you want to use a $50 or $100 increment to get the bidding high quickly.

If an item is not going well, the auctioneer may want to use a lower increment of only $25 or even $15 to keep the bidding alive and try to milk the item for as much as it can generate.

When coming up with a minimum or opening bid for silent and live auction items, price the item at less than half of what you estimate the retail value to be. Start with 40 percent of retail, and if that's too high, come down. For example, if a haircut in a salon would be $40, the minimum bid for this item should be $15. For a two-hour estate planning session, which might cost $250 on the outside, price it at $60 for the minimum bid.

Also consider how desirable an item may be. The more desirable, the higher the minimum bid should be. For less desirable items select a minimum bid as low as 75 percent off retail. Remember, you want to sell everything. Any money you can generate from a donation is pure profit, even if it is much less than you anticipated. Start to selectively reduce the minimum bids of silent auction items that are not receiving any bids about 40 minutes after silent auction begins. You may slash the opening by half to get the bidding started. If the items are not going, you priced them too high.

THE AUCTION CATALOG

The catalog, a photocopied, numbered list of all the auction items, except bazaar table items, is an important selling tool. Since there are no pictures, the catalog describes all the silent and live auction items in enough detail to make them enticing.

List all the donors in the catalog, so it also becomes a place to give recognition to everyone who made a donation. The timing of the catalog is important.

You should get the catalog distributed at least a week before the auction, so people can read in advance what's being auctioned off. I always go through the catalog and make check marks next to the items I am interested in bidding on. That way I can be focused at the auction and get what I want.

Put the most prized and expensive items in the live auction. Select the two live auction items you think will generate the most bidding. Put one of these items first and one last, to keep people there until the end.

The opening bid should be much higher for live auction items than for silent auction items. Be aware that some people may have feelings about their donations ending up in the silent auction instead of the live. They may be angry and feel unimportant. It is necessary to explain in advance that decisions to put donations in live or silent auction are not made based on the person but based on where the committee thinks the item or service will generate the most money.

Sometimes, you may have to put something in the live auction to appease a big donor. Don't worry about it. Just do it and be happy.

CATALOG TIMING

Donors tend to be "last minute Louies;" so there will always be additional items that come in after the catalog has been printed and distributed. Print an addendum as late as two days before the auction, showcasing the items that came in late. You can accept fabulous items at the auction itself.

We send the catalog home in the backpacks of the children whose parents have bought tickets in advance. Some catalogs are also available at the auction for people who decide to pay at the door.

CATALOG COPY

The catalog should be fun and have some tongue-in-cheek selling copy. But don't forget that you need to have a good, brief description of everything that comes with a package. Be accurate, even if something is not so great. You don't want bidders to be disappointed. Try to find an advertising copywriter among your parents who will write your catalog copy for free.

BANKING

The Role of the Treasurer

Treasurers are most important in this event. The treasurer and assistant treasurers should make the round of all the places where cash is being taken—like the bar, the grab bags, the bazaar table, the people selling the raffle tickets—and collect

money from them periodically. Do not leave people with big wads of cash throughout the evening.

Remember, some tables may need change during the course of the auction. At the grab bag table, we're always in need of fives and tens since so many people pay with twenty-dollar bills. The treasurers can be enormously helpful bringing change to people running tables or the bar. When you unload cash to the treasurer, be sure to get a receipt indicating how much money you have turned over. If the treasurer can't do it on the spot—and most can't, as they are much too busy—ask them to deliver the receipt when they bring you change.

You need to keep track of how much money your booth or table is making and have a written confirmation of how much money you have turned over to the treasures. This is just a simple safeguard to protect against confusion and misunderstandings.

Banking is a big job. You will need one banker for every 50 people, with a minimum of four. We need about ten people. Our auction draws about five hundred attendees and auctions off over three hundred items in the silent auction alone. If your auction is smaller, you may not need as many people in banking, but be sure to have enough. People don't like to wait in long lines to check out.

There are two basic banking methods: computerized or paper (manual). I will discuss both ways here. If you have someone who can handle a computer and owns a program like Excel that can create reports, then computerized banking may be the way to go. If you don't readily have someone who can do that, then use the paper or manual way. If you choose the manual method, you will need several big cartons to keep alphabetized auction vouchers and folders in—one for each attendee by paddle number. Here are the steps for banking.

BEFORE THE AUCTION

1. As vouchers with donations come in, they are given an item number and entered on a spreadsheet in Excel or a database program that can produce reports, such as Access. Include all the information on the voucher and don't forget the retail value. The retail value is important, so buyers can deduct any amount in excess of the retail they paid for an item from their taxes as a charitable contribution.

2. When the auction catalog is written, it becomes a shortened version of the spreadsheet.

3. Tie registration to banking. Each registrant gets a paddle number. Those same paddle numbers must

4. also be in the system tied to the name, address, and phone number of the person attending.

5. Bring a laptop computer with all the information,

spreadsheets, and so on to the auction.

- Be prepared for creative ideas from the auctioneer. Say the bidding is hot and heavy on a weekend house on the Italian Riviera in the live auction and the donor decides to be generous and offer a second weekend for the losing bidder. This is a great for the auction, but tough to handle for the banking people who now have to create a whole new item and put it in their database and award it to the proper bidder. Designate one volunteer to communicate and changes in the live auction to the bankers.

At the auction

Print each silent auction item on a sheet that has a duplicate or two carbon copies attached. This is necessary because when the silent auction bidding is closed, the sheet collectors take the top sheet to be organized by item number whether you're doing electronic banking or by paddle number in the paper system. The bottom sheet is left on the tables, so bidders can see which items they won.

1. Once the silent auction is over, the name and paddle number of the winning bidder must be entered into the system. Be careful *not* to transpose the paddle numbers and winning bids or someone might find himself or herself being charged $437 for a lunch with the music teacher she never bid on! Sheet collectors sort the top bidding sheets by item number for computerized banking or by paddle number for paper banking.

1. You should need only one data entry person. If the data is well organized, one person can handle the job. Using only one person will cut down on the number of mistakes like double entries. Once the data is entered, a report can be printed and

then the appropriate vouchers can be pulled and put in each folder by paddle number so when people come to checkout and pay for the items they've won, everything is in one place.

1. If you're using the paper method, you'll need three to five people pulling silent auction vouchers and putting them into folders. This can be a complex process and our school's Steve Russo, who ran banking for at least two years, recommends using the paper method for you first auction. Using the paper method makes it easier to completely understand the process.

1. Use your electronic report for bill preparation. Group the silent and live auction items by paddle number. Pull the certificates/envelopes for the items people won and put them in a folder marked with the winner's paddle number. Create a bill totaling all the items won and add it to the folder. Pass the folder to the cashier. You will need three to four people to pull certificates and envelopes.

You will need about five people matching up certificates and envelopes with the correct folders and handing them to cashiers. Use only two or three of your most trusted parents as cashiers taking money, especially cash. The majority of our parents pay by check or credit card.

-   Your voucher pullers will have to work like madmen to pull all the vouchers to get bills ready for those leaving after the silent auction. You have more time if you start pulling the bills for those who have remained for the live auction.

-   The two biggest crunches are right after the silent auction closes and after the live auction. Close banking for half an hour right after the live auction ends and the silent auction begins. This gives you time to gather all the items, set up bills, and make paying run much quicker and smoother.

RECONCILIATION

1. This is done after everyone has paid and gone home—except you! Count out your cash and give it to the treasurer. We like to do this more than once during the evening so the money does not sit in on place too long, tempting fate.

In our parents association closet, we had a special safe that can take deposits without being opened up and keep them secure. There is a big slot in the top, and the deposit drops into a drum. You rotate the handle, and the deposit is dumped into the body of the safe. If you have a setup like this in your school, deposit cash in the safe regularly so it doesn't get stolen lying around. Keep track of all the receipts for cash you turned over to the treasurer.

1. Keep a record of each and every check and credit card. Your bill forms should have a carbon copy for the PA so you can keep track of the payment information.

1. Check and see who won items and didn't pay for them or didn't pick them up at all. There will always be someone who couldn't wait in line because they had to get home to the babysitter. An electronic system is ideal for this step as it can run a report of all unclaimed items.

A paper system is more complicated since it involves collecting the vouchers, envelopes, and actual items still left, and sorting them out by paddle number. Next you will need to make calls and collect money. You will become a mini collection agency. Most people do pay up. If anyone says that they no longer want an item they won, let them off the hook. You can offer the item to the number-two bidder. If the number-two bidder doesn't want it, try number three. If you can't sell it to any of the bidders, sell it through your newsletter, at another event, or give it to a hardworking volunteer or deserving teachers as a reward. It really isn't worth it to try to force the winning bidder to pay for something he or she doesn't want. People get carried away and sometimes make mistakes.

Be generous about it. Out of an average 250 to 300 silent auction items only 10 to 15 usually will have to be collected.

VOLUNTEERS

- Have a floater or two who can get drinks or food for workers like the massagers, the palm reader, and the people manning the grab bag and bazaar tables. Floaters can relieve people to go bid or go to the bathroom. Floaters can solve problems and locate the auction chiefs in any emergencies.
- Each committee needs volunteers. Here is a suggested breakdown by committee:

- Location—Location selection should be done by the chairs of the event.
- Sponsors—The chairs usually find auction sponsors, but you can have a subcommittee handle this job.
- Food—This committee needs to find a good caterer who will do all the serving in addition to supplying the food. You will still need people to remove plates, unless you can talk the caterer into doing that, too, for the same price.
- Publicity—One or two good people are enough.
- Auctioneers—You will need three to four auctioneers; if you hire a professional, you only need one.
- Hiring a professional auctioneer who is paid on a percentage basis will increase the amount of money you will take in, but might not be as much fun as a parent volunteer.

- Live auction—One person to work with chairs creating live auction packages. Two spotters to call out and record paddle numbers of winning bidders.
- Silent auction—Two people to make up the silent auction bidding sheets. Four people to collect and sort bidding sheets after bidding is closed.
- Bazaar table—One person to price items, and three people to sell at the table at the auction.
- Grab bags—One person to solicit donations. Two or three to make up bags. Three to sell bags at the auction.
- Decorations/setup—Combine this committee with the setup committee. The two decorating committee chairs design and purchase the decorations and the setup volunteers put everything in place. You will need about five volunteers for this combined committee.
- Local canvassers—This committee needs a large group of volunteers. For best coverage, you need ten to twelve canvassers unless you live in a small town.
- Canvassers are volunteers who solicit donations for the silent and the live auction by asking retail stores, restaurants, and local businesses for contributions of items or services.
- Setup—Make this part of the decorating committee.
- Cleanup—If you're using a venue outside of the school, inquire about a cleanup fee. If you're using the school, you'll need a cleanup committee and maybe a fee for your custodian. Or hire an outside cleaning service. A cleaning service relieves parent volunteers who are tired at the end of the evening from hauling, carting, and cleaning. There are too many loose ends to take care of at the end of the auction to be hassled by cleanup.

- Banking—At a professional auction, the attendees leave their credit card imprint at check-in when they pick up their paddle. That way, at the end of the auction, the banking people add up their purchases and put it on the credit card and the buyer only has to look over the charges and sign the credit card slip.

- ○ People who do well under pressure are best for data entry and sheet separators.

- The people pulling items will have to work quickly together. Select your people well: people with a sense of humor and who thrive under a bit of craziness do well with this job.
- The best personality type for cashiers is the orderly type, who can make checkout faster. If you wait until the end to add up everything, it can take a long time to check out when the auction is over. Of course, people can leave early, but those who stay to the end won't wait as long if you're organized.
  - ○ Have some entertainment at the very end of the auction, like live music or old gold records to entertain people while they are waiting in line to pay.

- Donations—This committee sends out auction donation voucher forms with a photocopied suggested donation instruction sheet attached.
  - ○ Request all donations be mailed or delivered to the school office.
  - ○ Store the auction items in school closets, empty offices, or the basement of a volunteer.
- Tickets—This committee only needs a few volunteers. You need two people to sell tickets in advance and two people to sell tickets at the door. After the first two hours of the auction, everyone has arrived and this position is no longer needed.
- The donors are the biggest group of volunteers. You need as many as you can get. People can donate more than one item,

too. The more items you have, the more productive and fun your auction will be since more people will be able to go home winners.

DECORATION

Make things elegant: beautiful tablecloths, sleek bags for grab bags (not brown paper lunch bags), soft lighting, and color-coordinated decorations.

- Use a coat rack and clips to display large items, like quilts and afghans.
- Have a card, a designed computer printout, or photograph to display for each service offered. A picture of the donor with a resume that explains the person's qualifications makes the item seem more substantial. For example, we had a picture of the mother and her resume to show her Julliard schooling and experience to back up her offer of piano lessons.
- Display brochures of hotels where rooms are offered. Show the work of a photographer who is offering a photoshoot or video of your next party.

- Balloons are easy inexpensive decoration. Get silver or gold and black balloons and helium. Anchor a cluster at each table. Balloons lend a festive air.

HOW MUCH MONEY WILL YOU RAISE?

The auction may be the biggest moneymaking event you have. It's right up there in the thousands of dollars, along with he Street Fair and the Pledge Drive.

Your income will depend on how many items you have to sell, how much money your parents are willing to part with and how well run the event is.

If you start small and build, you'll be surprised at how quickly this event becomes the favorite of the parents, and a steady, reliable money-maker for the PA.

TIMELINE

You can put an auction together in a shorter timeframe, especially if you hold the event at your school. This is the ideal timeline:

One year ahead
Select the site and put down a deposit.
Five months ahead
Select committee heads.
Four months ahead
Recruit volunteers for the committees.
Three months ahead
Start publicity.
Set up banking software spreadsheets.
Committees swing into action.
Request donations.
As donations come in, begin data processing by putting the items on a computer (even if you will use paper for creating bills).

<u>Two months ahead</u>
Design and print invitations
Design decorations.
<u>One month ahead</u>
Continue data processing.
Pile on the publicity.
Increase pressure for more donations.
Distribute invitations by either email or snail mail.
<u>Three weeks ahead</u>
Begin putting parents' information on computer.
Make live auction packages.
Determine what goes in silent auction.
Start catalog copy.
Sell tickets at drop-off and pick-up at school.
<u>Two weeks ahead</u>
Print catalog.
<u>One week ahead</u>
Distribute catalog.

ACKNOWLEDGEMENT

Saying "thank you" is important in fund-raising. Although you don't need to send thank-you notes to the parents, you will need to send them to all companies that contribute, especially if you want to ask for those contributions again next year. If your school is large, this will be a big task and you may need a committee just to issue thank-you notes.

It's easiest to send a thank-you note when each donation comes in. This could keep one person busy for a few weeks. Mailing or emailing notes at receipt is a lot less daunting than attempting to send out three hundred the day after when everyone is exhausted.

Set up the notes in advance with return address and an opening or closing paragraph that you can use for each one. This way you only have to personalize one short central paragraph where you mention the actual donation.

Make a list of each item on an Excel spreadsheet, include the contact name, address, and phone number of the donor. Check off when the note goes out. Use this list the following year to solicit the same donors again.

NEW IDEAS

Make your auction an entertaining event by adding fun activities, such as massages, a palm reader, or games. Hire actors to dress up as palm readers or use parent volunteers. Parent massage-therapist volunteers can bring their massage chairs and set up. They can charge $10 for five minutes. (You need at least two massage chairs since this will be popular.)

Games with nice donated prizes can raise money and make your event livelier. Set up adult games, like darts, ring toss, or pick-a-number. Prizes could be leather change purses, CD holders, small kitchen wares, paperback books, CDs, pocket calendars, memo pads, address books, journals, small pocket tools, and other little items.

The pick-a-number game works this way. One person picks a number from one to twenty and writes it down on a slip of paper. Four people on the other side of the table pay $2 or $3 to guess the number. Each one picks a number, no two the same. The winner gets a prize.

For ring toss, the player who lands three rings on spikes set up on the floor, wins a prize. Charge $5 a try ($1 per ring tossed).

Or put together a darts game with balloons. The person who bursts the balloon, gets whatever prize it represents. The balloons are tied to a rolled-up piece of paper that is a certificate or information about the prize.

Children are not the only ones who like to play simple carnival games. Games will lend a sense of fun to the event—one or two are enough and won't overwhelm the auction or keep people from visiting, eating, and bidding!

Sell tickets to the game booths to avoid too much cash floating around. For your massage tables, palm reader, and grab bags, sell tickets at a central table. Then each special service collects the correct number of tickets required. For example: two $5 tickets for a massage, one for a palm reading, and four for a grab bag.

JUST STARTING OUT?

You can have a fine auction and raise lots of money even if you're just starting out. Here are some suggestions for schools just beginning to get their fund-raising off the ground and who don't have a lot of money to spend:

1. Have the auction in the school. You won't have to pay a space rental fee. Have the food and the silent auction in the cafeteria and the live auction in the auditorium or the gym, with chairs set up and standing room at the back.

2. Have a "penny auction" with a potluck dinner. A "penny auction" is when items are put on a table and a brown paper lunch bag, with the item's name on it, is set beside each one.

Sell raffle tickets. Parents put the tickets they buy in the bags of the items they want. After everyone has put in their tickets and dinner is finished, pull a ticket from each bag and award the

3. item to the winner. This type of auction creates excitement as no one knows who will win each item.

4. Have a potluck dinner so you don't have to charge admission. Or get food donations from local restaurants or tastings from several restaurants who want publicity.

5. Solicit donations from local restaurants and other merchants for free goods and services. Dinner for two or lunch for four will bring in money in a silent or live auction.

6. Ask for donations of goods and services from the parents in your school. Persuade people—everyone has something they can offer. The auction doesn't have to be all about things but can involve services, too. Parents might consider donating:

- cooking lessons
- dinner for two at their house or delivered to your house
- one month's dog-walking service
- dog bath and brushing
- lawn mowing for a month
- snow shoveling for a month
- errand running for a month
- power tools lessons
- make your own bookshelf (birdhouse, toy chest, etc.)with a carpenter
- tutoring kids for a month
- two Saturday nights of baby-sitting
- piano or any other musical instrument lessons
- sewing lessons
- knitting/crocheting lessons

- homemade afghan
- homemade quilt to order with your fabric selections
- three hours of word processing or editing or resume writing
- picking up your kids at school every day for two weeks.
- tennis, golf, swimming, or riding lessons
- bridge, gin rummy, pinochle, bid whist, or poker lessons
- garden work: planting, weeding, harvesting for two weeks
- car service to wherever you wish for a day

The list is endless!

1. Have a small but wonderful and creative live auction. You might consider getting the following donations from parents and local businesses: week or weekend at someone's vacation home. Or:

- lunch with a local celebrity
- membership at a local club or camp
- displaying your art at a local art gallery
- a beautiful piece of art donated by a local artist
- art done by the kids in school
- dinner for two or four donated by a local restaurant
- two nights donated from a nearby hotel
- tour of a television or radio station
- tour of a newspaper plant or candy factory And on and on. It all depends upon what is available in your community and what resources your fellow parents have.

AND DON'T FORGET...

- Bring blank certificates to be filled in for anything that's missing or forgotten or for donations that are made on the spot.
- Hold a post mortem meeting to discuss what worked and what didn't work at the auction. Getting everyone's opinion can help to make things smoother and more profitable next year.
- Write up all the procedures you use for the auction and put them in a loose-leaf binder to hand to the auction committee chairs the following year. This saves meeting time and duplication of effort.

SPRING EVENTS

Car Wash

WHAT IS A CAR WASH?

The students and their families wash cars for a fee. It can happen on the school campus or on a street closed off for this purpose.

HOW DOES A CAR WASH WORK?

This event is easy for schools that have a campus. Having a circular driveway helps. The children and their parents was cars for $5 or $10 per car. Or you can do it for a donation.

You need at least one hose with a nozzle control. Two is because being able to wash or rinse two cars at once will speed up the process. Also gather buckets, extra-large sponges, plenty of old towels or a huge supply of paper towels, garbage bags, mild soap—like dishwashing liquid—and plenty of energetic children. Make sure you have several places where you can connect hoses.

Add to that a warm day—because everyone involved in this will be soaked to the skin by the time it's over.

Set up an entrance where cars come in and an exit where they leave. A parking lot with an entrance and an exit so cars can move through and make room for more cars is ideal. This can be done in the city, if you get a permit to use the block your school is on. You can have cars coming in at one end of the street and exiting, clean as whistle, at the other.

Make red Stop signs and use tape to mark the stop lines in key areas, like the payment booth, wash, dry, and rinse areas. Make 5 m.p.h. speed limit signs and place them where drivers can see them.

Divide your path into four sections: waiting area, washing area, rinsing area, and drying area. You may choose to eliminate drying. People don't want to wait, so you need plenty of volunteers to move cars though quickly. The waiting area is where you take the money.

The washing area needs the most space to keep things moving. Keep the rinsing and drying areas small, since those functions take the least amount of time.

You need several big signs. If you intend to have this event every year, then it is worthwhile to invest in large banners advertising the car wash. If you don't have the funds to buy two big banners this year, make big signs by hand using poster paper. Five or ten dollars is reasonable to charge. There is very little monetary outlay here, except for the signs, soap, and towels.

Schedule the car wash on a Saturday in the afternoon, when the sun is the strongest and the air is the warmest. Lunchtime to late afternoon is a good time to run a car wash, since you'll catch many people out running errands. Four hours should be enough to discover how it will work for you. That is enough time to soak and exhaust everyone involved.

Try to get your car wash mentioned on local radio. So many people listen to radio in their cars that it is the perfect medium for car wash advertising, and might drive impulse traffic to your car wash.

Call the community affairs or program directors of your local radio stations. For mention in your local newspaper, go to their website and under the "contact us" section, you will find instructions for submitting information about your upcoming community events.

VOLUNTEERS

You need managers, publicity people, and lots and lots of workers: washers, rinsers, dryers, and people to take the money. Divide the day into crews of people who will work for one hour. For a four-hour event, you will need four crews.

Each crew could consist of two money takers, six washers, two rinses, and two dryers. Figure out in advance how many cars you can get into your space to wash at one time.

Washing will require at least two people per car, one on each side. Rinsing can be one person per car, and drying will require two per car, again one for each side. This will tell you how many people you will need for each crew.

You will need volunteers to make sure drivers are obeying all the stop signs and proceeding slowly. Choose a volunteer for each stop sign. Have alternates ready to give them a break.

SECRETS TO SUCCESS

If your school is located near a main drag or highway, you will have a better chance at attracting more cars. If you are located off on a side street somewhere so people will have to drive out of their way to get to you, it will be harder to attract customers. Put banners on the main streets with arrows leading to your car wash.

One way you can boost the number of customers is to align yourself with a civic organization. If you can get the sponsorship of the Rotary, Elks, Lions, or other fraternal organization, they will get the word out and increase your number of customers dramatically.

A fraternal organization may also make a small donation or pay for your banners as part of their sponsorship. Perhaps a store, or even a gas station, will sponsor your event. Look for members of these organizations among your parents or grandparents to provide initial contact. Or call your local organization and ask for the name of their community liaison.

You might consider charging $5 for wash only and $10 for wash and dry. Add waxing to increase your revenue if you have enough volunteers. Sell coffee, cake, or hot dogs to waiting car owners to boost your profits.

HOW MUCH MONEY WILL YOU RAISE?

You can raise several hundred dollars if you have help in generating publicity and are located near a busy street. If you get sponsorships, that will mean more money, too.

TIMELINE

<u>End of previous year</u>

Set a date for the event.

Recruit volunteers.

<u>One week ahead</u>

Buy supplies.

The Book Fair

WHAT IS A BOOK FAIR?

A book fair is a sale of children's books through one company that takes place on the school grounds, through a mail order catalog, in a bookstore, or even online for a "virtual" book fair. Book fairs promote reading and boost literacy.

Scholastic Books carries both their own books and books from 150 other publishers and will bring them to your school. They are the leader in book fairs; they deliver more than 140,000 fairs worldwide. You can reach Scholastic online at https://bookfairs.scholastic.com/bookfairs/landing-page.html

Scholastic has a great selection of instructional nonfiction and reference books, including books on parenting.

Barnes and Noble will create a book fair either in your school or in one of their stores, that will benefit your school. For details, check out their book fair website here: https://www.barnesandnobleinc.com/our-stores-communities/bookfairs/

Book fairs do not require any money up front, so they are ideal as fund-raisers for schools just starting fund-raising programs.

HOW DOES AN ON-SITE BOOK FAIR WORK?

The book company brings portable bookcases that fold together, so the books can be safely stored at night in the school. The books arrive in boxes. PA volunteers set up the shelves with books according to age, reading level, or grade level in the school lobby. Scholastic gives you other items to sell too, including bookmarks, CDs, writing equipment, software, and posters.

Although their service leaves something to be desired, because you may not be able to get all the books you want and getting supplies replenished quickly is not automatic, they are knowledgeable and experienced in the art and science of the school book fair. The percentage discount the school gets depends upon the plan or tier you select.

Check out Barnes and Noble and compare what they offer to Scholastic and pick the company that works best for your school.

Approach your local bookstore. Chances are they'd be happy to create a book fair for your school and offer you a generous percentage for the additional sales. Avoid a ton of

work by having the fair in the store. They will be thrilled at the increased traffic and sales.

If you use a local store, you can have more control over the books offered. Sit down with the store manager and work together to create a fantastic book fair you can repeat every year.

Be sure to cover book selection, replenishing sellouts, selling tips, and ideas with your bookstore rep. Be careful when you select your representative at Scholastic. The right rep can help you get a better selection of books and give you faster service with reorders.

Reorder books that have sold out while the book sale is in progress, so you can capitalize on a book's popularity. Scholastic picks up leftover books and other items when the fair is over. Be sure to establish that the school is not responsible for unsold books or other items.

WHAT ARE THE STEPS FOR AN ON-SITE BOOK FAIR?

First you must get in touch with Scholastic,

Barnes and Noble, or your local bookstore. Examine all their purchase discount tiers or plans. Select the one that is right for your school and make a deal. Book selection is key to the success of the fair. "Our parents always look for Caldecott, Newberry, and Coretta Scott King award-winning books," one book fair chair says.

Although Scholastic does the book selection, take an active role and request certain books you know will sell to your parents. Perhaps your librarian or experienced teachers can help select books.

SCHEDULING

Schedule your book fair to start on a day or evening when you know parents are going to be in the school. For example, if the kids are putting on a huge school play, have the book fair start during the run of the play. Set it up in the school lobby. Parents can browse before or after the show and during intermission.

Or schedule your book fair to coincide with your science fair or art show. Schedule your book fair before or during a basketball game or other sporting event that takes place in the gym. You can build a big fair right before Christmas. Adding games in the gym, with a bake sale and pizza in the cafeteria.

Consider scheduling two book fairs, one in November during the fall parent/teacher conferences and one in March during the spring parent/teacher conferences. Parent/teacher conference night is a popular time to schedule a book fair. Make sure you lock in your date early as the publisher maybe swamped with book fairs at that time.

Parents in the school pass by the fair on their way in and on their way out of school to meet with their child's teacher. Not all parents buy books, but you'll get higher sales because it's hard to walk away without buying something. The November sale comes right before Christmas. Holiday purchases boost sales.

Consider starting your book fair to run only two days. If it's successful, stretch it a few days or ever to a full week next time. Having the book sale for a week allows teachers to sign up to bring their classes down to the sale so the kids can buy books of their own choosing. Post a sign-up sheet in the school office for teachers to bring their classes to the fair. Remind teachers to tell parents which day their child is going to the fair, so the kids have money to buy books.

Publicity is vital. You must get the word out to your parents that you're having the fair and where and when it's being held.

Promote the sale in your school newsletter. Put up signs both in the school and on the front door, send flyers home in the children's backpacks.

VOLUNTEERS

If you can find a parent who loves books and is knowledgeable about them, grab him or her and hope they stay with this job for a long time. Keeping someone to chair this event for more than one year is important so you don't have to reinvent the wheel every year. It's easier to run a smooth, profitable event if you have an experienced chair and returning volunteers.

Divide coverage into shifts. Pull in two volunteers for each shift. Volunteers answer questions, help people find books, and keep an eye on the cash box at the same time. If you run five shifts each day, you need ten volunteers per day. If you run the book fair for five days, you'll need at least fifty volunteers. The chairman of the event should also be there most of the day, every day if possible.

SECRETS OF SUCCESS

One secret is to have the book fair on conference night. It is the only time during the year every single parent comes to the school. This may not be true in your school. Perhaps other events draw more parents.

Another idea to help stock classrooms with books is to have teachers create book wish lists. The event chair can get a list of the available books in advance and pass it along to the teachers. Publicize the classroom wish lists. Parents can select a book or two from the list to contribute.

A bright-colored plastic bin with the teacher's name on the front can hold books bought from that teacher's list. As a parent buys a book, they move it to the bin. This way, parents know which books have been bought and which are left.

To encourage the purchase of books for the classroom, give the parents a small stick-on bookplate for each book they buy. They put their child's name on the plate and stick the plate inside the book. Everyone will know you have given books to the classroom and your child garners a little status for having contributed. Ask the school librarian to create a wish list and use bookplates for the books on that list, too.

Most schools run book fairs before the holidays. It may be harder to get the best books right before the holidays since many schools are doing this at the same time. You might do better in spring with a better book selection.

HOW MUCH MONEY WILL YOU RAISE?

Book fairs are not the biggest moneymaking events. However, depending on the size of your school, you can make hundreds to thousands of dollars. If you're not doing much in the way of fund-raising, the book fair may produce even more for your school. This is a fairly uncomplicated event to produce that requires no dollar outlay up front. Parents understand the need for books in school.

TIMELINE

End of previous year

Select your publisher and lock in event date or dates.

At the start of the year

Recruit fifty volunteers.

Put the fair or fairs on the calendar in your school newsletter.

One month before the fair

Remind volunteers. Get wish lists from teachers.

Two weeks before the event

Start heavy duty publicity in newsletter and in school.

JUST STARTING OUT?

A book fair is an excellent fund-raiser if your school is just starting out. No up-front money is required. Though the profit margin is not big, with enough parents, teachers, and grandparents buying books, your school can raise a good sum to launch other fund-raising activities.

Local Author Event

WHAT IS A LOCAL AUTHOR EVENT?

You'd be surprised how many authors live in your city or neighboring towns. These professionals crave a place to showcase and sell their work. The school is perfect for an author book signing and sale.

HOW DOES AN AUTHOR BOOK SIGNING WORK?

Remember those long folding tables I suggested you buy? Here's another event that requires those. Your PA invites authors and/or artists to participate in the show. You charge each one a fee for use of the space, table, and publicity.

Figure out how many tables you can fit comfortably in your schoolyard, parking lot, or both. Draw up a diagram of each table, to scale, so you'll have the exact number that fit. Either buy two chairs for each table or borrow chairs from the school. Classroom chairs may be too small and too low to work with the tables.

Charge $40-$70 per table—maybe more if you have two authors sharing one. Put out the news of the event by word-of-mouth, on social media, in your newsletter, and by hanging posters in the school and in local businesses, like restaurants, grocery stores, and cafés.

Create an online event at http://www.eventbrite.com or any of the many other websites that offer that service. Have authors fill out forms which include information on the genre of books they are selling. Create an event for authors of adult fiction, nonfiction, and even children's books to appeal to the widest audience possible.

Receive payment by check, credit card, or set up a PayPal account. Many authors prefer PayPal.

VOLUNTEERS

You won't need many volunteers to run this event. Here's a quick list:

- Event chair

- Set-up crew (set up tables & chairs)
- Knock-down crew (return tables & chairs)
- Publicity (two volunteers)
- Organization (two volunteers to work with the chair at the event to check off authors, send them to the proper tables, and troubleshoot)
- Security

SECRETS TO SUCCESS

Make extra money by having one table reserved for a PA bake sale. Have finger foods like cookies and cupcakes plus coffee and bottles of water.

HOW MUCH MONEY WILL YOU RAISE?

You might need to price your tables low, at about $35 the first year you do this. You need to make sure to have plenty of publicity. Send press releases to the local media, shout it out on social media. Post it in store and restaurant windows. The more people who buy books, the higher the price you can charge for a table the following year.

How many tables can you set up in your schoolyard? Ten, fifteen, twenty? The more tables, the more money you'll make. If you can find twenty authors and have room for twenty tables, you'll make a minimum of $750.00. Once this event catches on, you can raise the price of the tables.

Twenty tables at $50 each will bring you $1,000. Not bad for a low-effort event. Put the most energy into advertising. You need to draw readers who are willing to buy books. If you don't have a big crowd and the authors don't sell books, this event will fizzle and not become a steady even you can count on every year. So put out the P.R. – flyers in stores, in libraries, advertising the list of authors who will be available for signing.

Send out the list of participating authors in your newsletter to alert parents who might be fans. Send a press release to the local radio stations and newspapers. The more publicity you get, the bigger the success of the event.

The one catch is you have to have the money to invest in the tables if you can't borrow them from the school. Buying your own tables is a good investment for the PA, as there are so many occasions when you will use them.

TIMELINE

<u>End of previous year</u>
Set the date for the event.
Begin recruiting authors.
Publicize the event on social media and locally.
Put up a flyer in the library.
Call authors you know and begin word-of-mouth.
<u>Three months ahead</u>
Finalize your list of authors.
Begin publicity for the event.
Recruit volunteers.
<u>Day before the event</u>
Set up tables.
Print out list of authors and their tables.

JUST STARTING OUT?

You can do this event, even if you don't own tables or have the funds to buy them. Find out where you can rent tables. Negotiate a low rental rate. Add the rental cost to the price of the table rental. If the event attracts readers, authors will be willing to pay for the chance to showcase their books.

Use proceeds from this event to purchase tables, increasing your profit next year.

The Street Fair

WHAT IS A STREET FAIR?

A street fair takes place most often on a Saturday. A city permit allows the PA to close off the street and have a fair, which consists of food, game booths, secondhand books, toys, clothes, housewares, music, vendors, and rides (if affordable).

It's a huge party for the kids and an opportunity for creative ideas. A well-run street fair can bring a ton of money to the PA, create a strong sense of community, and provide a fun day for parents, children, and neighbors.

If your school has limited funds or no funds, check out the "Just Starting Out" section at the end of this chapter.

HOW DO YOU CREATE A STREET FAIR?

A street fair starts with the PA getting a permit to close the street for one Saturday each year. If your school has a sizeable campus, hold your fair on school grounds, eliminating the need for permission to close public streets. You can also set up in a football field, a gym, the cafeteria, or a spare parking lot (if you still have enough space left for cars to park).

Check with your city or town hall to see if you need a permit to conduct the fair. You may need a restaurant permit to cook and serve food. This permit details the required temperature of the grills and the safe handling of food by having workers wear gloves, caps, and so on.

Insurance coverage is necessary. Before you have your street fair, make sure the school's insurance company adds a rider to cover the street fair. Ride providers should have their own

insurance, too. Be sure to see proof of their insurance.

The first Saturday after Memorial Day weekend is a good time to schedule the fair. This can be the biggest event of the year and involve more people than any other event. Almost everyone can play some part in the street fair.

Fill your schoolyard or the street with fun, magic, rides, surprises, games, laughs, food, and just plain glee. Use all the space available. Fill your main yard with class booths around the perimeter, close to the fence. Use the center for your maze, if you have one. A petting zoo and trackless train can be situated on other parts of school property. Outside vendors hawking their wares can line your street.

CORPORATE SPONSORSHIP

Corporate sponsorship can turn a street fair into a big moneymaker. A street fair has some fixed expenses such as huge banners, food, rides, promotional materials, and more.

Stop at your local bank to request sponsorship. In return for their sponsorship, put "Sponsored by (your bank's name)" on banners, flyers, everything.

Many banks have community affairs budgets with funds to donate to local community projects every year. The trick is to get your request, in writing, to the right person early in the year, before their budget is totally allocated to other events. Often banks spend money to create goodwill in their communities.

Try fraternal organizations, big local stores, brokerage firms, law firms, and any other large, successful businesses in your neighborhood. Sponsorship ads seed money—necessary to making a big return on the street fair. Hard work and a sponsorship will take some of the pressure off and really boost your profit by minimizing outlay.

Also try to find sponsorships for specific booths, e.g. getting a local veterinarian or pet supply store to sponsor a petting zoo.

Look for a store or local business that would put up the funds to sponsor a ride or a manicure shop that might donate $150 toward supplies, or the actual supplies, for a manicure booth. Specific sponsorships give you the chance to have some booths or happenings you might not be able to afford otherwise.

Make sure to put a sign at each sponsored booth, giving credit to the store or local business. This will not only help build goodwill in the community but create a viable list of sponsors for the next year.

The fair can be put together in an endless variety of ways to match your community's interests and to keep it fresh every year.

Here are some examples to spark your imagination:

CLASS BOOTHS

Class booths have games or activities invented by each class and put side-by-side in a big blacktopped yard. Sometimes, all the classes in one grade unite and do something big, like sponsoring the petting zoo or finding a sponsor and running the booth. If they do, add a sign, giving the class credit for providing the booth.

Class parents collect money from the other parents in their class to buy supplies and prizes for the class booth. Depending upon the type of booth and the size of your class, contributions from $10 to $15 per child may be enough to fund the booth prizes.

Here are some examples of class booths:

- Cupcake decorating
- Doughnut eating—where donuts are hung by string and two kids compete to see who can eat the whole doughnut first without using hands—similar to bobbing for apples. This booth is ideal for corporate sponsorship by Dunkin' Donuts or Krispy Kreme.
- Ring toss—toss rings onto rubber spikes
- Knock down the milk cartons with a tennis ball
- Kids Jeopardy
- Guess-the-item—put household items in a pillowcase, blindfold the child, and have them guess what things are. Use items like: fork or spoon, bar of soap, small candlestick, candle, crayon, chalk, pencil, toothbrush, nail file, and a quarter.

- Wheel of chance
- Face painting
- Penny toss—toss pennies in small cups that float in a big tub of water
- Magnetic fishing—fishing using a magnet or string tied to a stick. The kids can make cardboard or paper fish (with metal paper clips through their noses) with numbers on them that correspond to prizes.
- Temporary tattoos
- Manicures with nail sticker
- Snow cone stand
- Lemonade stand
- Popcorn stand—rent or buy popcorn-making machine
- Create your own sand art
- Dunking booth—try to get the principal or gym teacher to be the one dunked.

All the game booths offer prizes. We usually get the prizes from the U.S. Toy Catalog or the Oriental Trading Company Catalog. Find these catalog companies online at www.ustoy.com[1] and www.oriental-trading.com[2]. Sometimes, discount stores also have good inexpensive small toys to use as prizes.

If you decide to pick out the prizes yourself, remember to select ones that appeal to both boys and girls. Here are some prize ideas: Pencils, rulers, compasses, magnifying glasses, tattoos, small plastic animals, fortune fish, tiny notebooks, palm-sized games, individually wrapped candy, plastic Dracula teeth.

Make sure every child receives some sort of prize. Make the games easy or have different prizes for different levels of achievement. My favorite is one where you knock down the milk cartons with a tennis ball,

---

a game you must put in a spot with a fence around it or you'll be chasing tennis balls all day! It's a simple booth that doesn't require much preparation, but it's always popular—maybe because kids love to throw things?

Charge two tickets for the booth and draw lines on the pavement with chalk to show where the kids should stand. Keep moving kids closer until they knock down the milk cartons. Everyone coming to this booth gets a prize. As a result, there's always a line of kids waiting.

Try to keep the prizes low at the class booths. A sand art booth, where kids create art by layering different colored sand in a small bottle, is the most expensive since the sand and bottles are costly. The cheaper the booth, the more activity you get and the more tickets you'll sell.

The committee chair running the class booths needs a well-drawn map of the schoolyard, the gym,

or wherever you plan to put the booths. Draw a floor plan and give each class booth a spot. Don't put booths with candy in a sunny spot. On the day of the fair, each class can find out where their booth is from the committee chair. There shouldn't be any confusion.

How do you get all the classes to comply and put together a booth? Class parents are good motivators. They are responsible for getting a class booth up and running. Sometimes, the teacher gets involved. She or he has the kids make the banner for the booth, or maybe even parts of the booth itself, in class. Sometimes, there are classes that cannot get it together and don't participate. That's not the end of the world. This is one area where the creativity of your parents and children can really run wild.

Charge from two to seven tickets, approximately, per booth. Sell tickets for 50¢ each. One hint to making your class booth really popular: the better your prizes are, the better the turnout at your booth will be.

THE MAZE

This idea got started when we had a parent who owned a moving company and donated huge boxes to the school. Someone came up with the idea of using the boxes to make a crawl-through maze and put it in the middle of the schoolyard during the street fair. Architect parents drew complicated plans and a crawl-through maze was fashioned out of the wardrobe moving boxes. The maze had a few breakthroughs or openings so the children could pop their heads out or parents could look into them for a lost child.

The maze was one of the most popular attractions of the street fair. For two or three tickets, kids disappeared for five minutes and crawled around in the dark like babies. When the kids of the parents who donated the boxes finally graduated after ten years at the school, we all mourned the passing of the maze.

GRAB BAGS

Although grab bags have been covered in the Harvest Festival chapter, the street fair is the major grab bag event where around 500 are sold. They are so popular they sell out before 3:00 p.p. This means selling about 125 bags per hour!

The contents of these grab bags are made up mainly from donations from corporations and parents who work at companies that have premiums. For example, one parent at the Environmental Protection Agency gave EPA pencils or small boxes of four crayons every year. McDonald's donated 500 toys every year. Corporate donations included key rings from a bank, pens from Empire Blue Cross, and mouse pads from the Children's Museum.

Insurance companies have giveaways. Fifty or a hundred of these can really help your grab bags. One year, our school got 100 reversible caps that were black on one side with the logo of the Syfy Channel and white on the other with the logo of the USA Network. The caps drove up grab bag sales, and we sold out in record time.

One parent who works for Colgate got us toothbrushes and little toothpaste sachets. One year, The Gap donated 500 small backpacks. Do you attend the Premium Incentive Show? You can pick up samples of all kinds of things there. On the last day, some people donated a lot—freeing them from having to pack it up and cart it home. Kids love this little stuff, even if it isn't toys.

California Tattoo always gave a generous donation of temporary tattoos at the Premium Show. If you don't go to the show, try contacting them directly here: https://californiatattoos.com/

Truly amazing!

When donations aren't quite enough, order from the U.S. Toy or Oriental Trading. I have frequently bought small magnifying glasses, American flag pins, or miniature Tootsie Rolls, items that would be good for boys or girls.

Try to mix up the bags and make them all a little different. It's better when you have 100 of this and 75 of that because it's easier to vary the bags. Buying assortments from the catalogs is great. If the bags are identical, why would anyone want more than one? We sell three, four, five, or more bags to one child because each one is a surprise and a little different. Repeat buyers make your school more money.

How much to charge depends on your school. I'd say $1.00 or $2.00. If your child goes wild and has to have three bags, make a deal – three bags for $5.00. The parents save a buck and the PA makes an extra three.

If you've collected some items that are too big to fit into those lunch bags, do not despair. Make "special prize" tickets out of neon-colored paper for the oversized items and put them in the grab bags. Write the name of the item on the prize ticket.

At the street fair, ask the kids, "Did you get a special prize ticket? Look inside." This drives the multiple sales. Kids come back, hoping for special prize tickets. The more special prizes you have, the better. It's not even the prize itself that most kids are after; it's the *winning* of the prize that is so important. The 3-for-$5. Deal will drive up sales. Parents might have a five-dollar-bill in their wallets –saves making change, too!

Grab bags need to be put together one or two days before the fair. We stuff brown paper lunch bags with our donated goodies and staple them closed so the contents don't fall out and kids can't peek inside them and choose based on the stuff they see.

Load the brown bags into huge, sturdy, black plastic garbage bags and store those in the school until the morning of the fair.

If you have five people to help stuff the bags, the task goes along quickly and should be completed in about three hours. For the grab bag table, we use three long tables joined together in the shape of a U. The three tables work best so you can store the grab bags under the tables and pull them out when the supply on the tables gets low. Special prizes need to be kept behind the table and out of sight.

Manning this table is the best job in the street fair. Some people come back year after year to do this job. To see the looks on the children's faces, their happiness is great. A street fair is about the kids, so if you get a child who doesn't have enough tickets or even no tickets, give them a grab bag anyway.

SECOND-HAND ROSE

This is a great section to sell all the white elephants that our parents can haul into the school. From toys to china sporting equipment to board games, and kitchenware, these tables are close to a garage sale.

Storage is the biggest problem with this booth. Can you get the use of a classroom before the event? Or a storage room? You need volunteers to price all items beforehand and throw out anything broken.

Group the items by type; all china items in one place, all board games together, all small toys together, and all kitchen items together. Put small items of about the same value in a box or basket, and put one price on the basket.

Be prepared to haggle. It's better to sell everything you have even at low prices than to throw out or give away anything. Your mission is to turn everything into cash.

BOOK TABLE

This is the most amazing section of the street fair. Get used children's and adult's books from your parents. Reach out to publishers for donations of new books. If you can drum up a good contact at a publishing house, you can clean up in the book department. Check your parent body for someone who works for a book publisher or bookstore.

Divide up the books into children's and adults. In the adult section, divide into hardcover and paperback. Then divide into categories the mysteries, biographies, cookbooks, parenting, science fiction, romance, how-to, coffee table books, and so on.

In the children's section, put all books of a series together, like all the Nancy Drew in one place, the Babysitter's Club in another. Parents are often looking for more books like their children's favorites.

Create separate prices for used books vs. new one.

New books go for various prices up to $5. Same old low prices for the secondhand books. As the day wears on, drop your prices so you can sell more books. You don't want to haul a ton of heavy books somewhere after the fair is over.

For the last hour of the fair, consider offering book buyers a shopping bag for $5 to fill with all the books they can fit in. It's a great way to get rid of books.

MASSAGE

If you have a professional massage therapist among your parents, or a pro who is willing to donate his or her services for a day, set up chairs at the street fair and offer a massage. Charge $10-$20 for ten minutes. This is a popular booth and will always be busy.

SECONDHAND CLOTHES

Secondhand clothes are a big draw. Running the secondhand clothes table is a big job, especially if you get a lot of donations. Although you ask that people donate only gently used clothing, you may get clothes you wouldn't put on your dog. Have a group of volunteers sort through the items.

Get volunteers to separate the good stuff into big bins for men, women, boys, and girls. Discard any clothing in bad shape. As a bonus for doing this thankless task, suggest to the head of this committee to let the sorters select a few items to buy before the fair.

A presale for all the parents in the school before the fair doesn't work for two reasons:

1. It's a lot of extra work getting people to cover the sale in the lobby the day before the street fair, using up good volunteers before the

event.

1. All the best clothing is pulled out before the fair, reducing interest in the clothing booth and diminishing sales the day of the fair. You need coat racks, hangers, and lots of plastic or paper bags. Hang up as much as you can so the clothes will be easy to look at and take up less table space. The better the display, the more the clothing will sell. Group clothing by

gender and for kids as much by size as you can, with infant and toddler sizes separate from the larger sizes.

2. Be ready to haggle here, too. The object is to get rid of the clothing, turning it into cash. Be willing to accept a lower price. The bag-of-books idea works here, too. As the fair wears on, you might offer an all-you-can-stuff-in bag of clothing for $5.

SCHOOL TABLE

A school table serves many functions. It's where raffle tickets are sold. It is where school-designed T-shirts are sold, and it is the table that disseminates material about your school. It's the perfect place to have veteran parents available to greet incoming kindergarten parents.

This central table is where everything originates and where you can find the PA heads most of the day. Send an invitation to the street fair to the incoming kindergarten parents and direct them to this table. The incoming parents find it welcoming to be able to talk with current parents face-to-face.

Have a raffle with terrific prizes. Sell the tickets at the school table but also have roving raffle-ticket sellers hawking tickets throughout the fair. Typical raffle prizes are bicycles, televisions, and even dinner for two at a popular restaurant. The raffle can raise $500+ pretty quickly and with little fuss.

Create special street fair T-shirts with your street fair logo. These shirts sell quickly. Have a design-the-T-shirt contest for students at the beginning of the year. Buy shirts in a large quantity to get the lowest price. Mark them up by a few dollars to make money for the PA. Look for a local T-shirt silkscreen printer to get a good price or find one online. Try www.epromos.com[3].

---

3.   http://www.epromos.com

Use http://www.iprint.com or a similar service on the Internet to print your T-shirts using four-color art. Call and negotiate a special rate. Be persuasive and get a low price.

FOOD

Food is a big part of the fair and is provided several ways:

The Grill

Set up a grill to cook hot dogs and hamburgers. Rent an "industrial-strength" 3' x 6' grill instead of something small and flimsy. Sell cold soda and water there, too. Get your supplies at discount beverage stores. To sell beer, you may need a special liquor permit.

Bake Sale

Have a bake sale with homemade goodies, from brownies to cookies and cupcakes to whole cakes. Approach local bakeries for donations of loaves of peasant and whole grain bread. These loaves are big sellers and jack up revenue from the bake sale, since you charge much more for them than you do for a brownie or cupcake.

Buffet

Do you have a multicultural parent body? Encourage them to make food from their heritage for the street fair. The PA can buy the food and have them cook it, maybe even starting the night before. Set up long tables for food and picnic tables for diners as if it were a potluck. Can you get the food donated?

Even better. Rent professional-size chafing dishes from a local caterer for steaming pans of Jamaican chicken, beans, and rice, and homemade chili, or whatever is native for your parents.

The exotic foods send enticing odors through the air. This is the best advertising, as the wonderful smells bring in hungry families. We charge per plate, and people fill them up along the buffet line as they wish. Charge $5.00 or $10.00 per plate, whatever works.

MUSIC

Get a few parents who are musicians to play for

an hour or so at the fair. Set them up where the food is being served, so people can listen while they eat. Everything from country music to cool jazz works.

Why music? Music draws people to your fair and to the food stands; it's a great advertisement. Keep the music at the proper level, though, so people can sit and listen without being blasted out of their seats. Also, if the music is too loud, it drowns out necessary conversation.

RIDES

Rides are a big attraction at any street fair, but the

rides are expensive to rent. You may not make a profit on the rides unless you have corporate sponsorship for them or charge higher prices. But rides do attract customers, so they are worth it. Rides that take more kids are more likely to make money. For example, the castle bounce—that big inflated thing that looks like a castle that kids climb on and bounce around for a while—can take about eight kids at a time whereas a ride like the rock wall can only be climbed by one child at a time.

Search "amusement rides" online for companies that provide rides for fairs. Some companies will not charge for a rented ride if the fair is rained out.

This is a very important feature to look for when you select a ride company. With rides costing hundreds to thousands of dollars, it's crucial insurance to have a company that will give you a credit for a rain date.

Most companies charge in advance. Some may get paid when they deliver the ride. When selecting rides, please take into account the space you plan to use. Get the dimensions in advance for each ride you're interested in, including the height. Height is important if there are any trees in the area you will be using.

You can't wait until the day of the fair when the rides are delivered to discover a ride doesn't fit into a space earmarked for it. You need to have a floor plan with accurate dimensions and then sit down and plot out the places the rides will fit in.

Also you will need to know if a ride needs electricity so that you can locate it near a plug. If a power source isn't available, rent rides that come with generators. Rides are powered by either gas generators or noisy electric fan generators.

Check with your company to find out the electrical requirements. If they are bringing a fan generator, ask how noisy it is. Many fan generators are as noisy as a lawn mower. This may distract from the enjoyment of the ride, so a gas generator may be preferable.

Rides are delivered on large trucks. Make sure you know when the truck will be arriving and that you have mapped out a route for the truck that will be clear when it arrives. If you will have vendors, make sure their goods are not blocking the path of the rides truck.

Charge for the rides at a projected breakeven. Figure out how much you have to charge by the price of the ride and the number of hours the fair will be open. That should give you what you need to charge people to break even or make a profit.

Some of the most popular rides have been:

- The castle-bounce
- The trackless train
- The swing, which can take about twenty kids at a time so you can make a lot of money.

Make the most of the rides by placing concession stands adjacent to where the lines for the popular rides will be. This is how Disney World makes so much money. Cotton candy, lemonade, hot dogs, or cookies being sold next to the line of a popular ride will do well. Check with your ride companies and get a date when you have to book the rides. In New York City, we needed to book the rides a few months in advance.

In other communities, the lead time may be different. Remember, when you book, you will need to pay a deposit.

Planning involves selecting ride companies and rides, choosing appropriate spots to put rides where they will fit easily and leave room for a line of children waiting to get on, and lining up. Usually, the ride company will provide one person to run the ride—such as the engineer to drive the train—and that's all.

You will need to check and make sure that a person who knows how to work the ride will be included as part of your deal. You'll need volunteers to keep lines straight.

Better to plan to have to many parents helping on the rides rather than not enough. So if this is your first year, round up as many parents as you can. You can offer the running of a ride to a class instead of a class booth.

Some rides need more volunteers than others. For example, the trackless train needs several volunteers. Each car on the trackless train has a little door. Parent volunteers need to be there to help children off the trains and help other children on. Don't leave this up to parents of kids riding as they will swing their children right on ahead of others, and it'll be chaos.

Set up time slots of one hour for each ride and get at least two volunteers for each time period. That way if someone doesn't show up, at least you have one volunteer and time to recruit another.

If people know they only have to put in an hour, it'll be easier to recruit them. If one-hour times slots don't work, try half an hour. Half-hour time slots require more supervisors, but if it gets people to step up and volunteer, then you'll be more successful.

Consider offering a $20 or $30 "ride bracelet" for kids that allows kids to ride all the rides as many times as they want. You may not be able to charge quite as much in your community. An unlimited-ride bracelet can reduce arguments with kids who may want to go on the rides again and again, and at $2 per ride the parents may have to put their foot down.

Rides are a blast; the little kids really love them. They can be moneymakers, directly or by boosting attendance. Either way, they add excitement to your fair.

VENDORS

Vendors are essential to a good fair and a very easy way to make money. Vendors are outside merchants selling items not related to the school or the fair. The school makes money by renting space in a special spot. Charge by the space at $50 or $60 for a small space, and up to $80 or $100 for a large space.

Vendors must operate under certain restrictions. Do not accept vendors with alcohol. Do not accept any food vendors, except perhaps an ice cream truck. Food vendors compete with your own food sales. Do not accept any other vendors that compete with products you are selling, such as books or secondhand clothes.

Do not accept vendors who sell seriously overpriced merchandise. You don't want your customers to be cheated by a vendor. Create a contract with vendors specifying what items they cannot sell, for example, don't allow vendors to sell those poppers that explode when kids throw them on the ground.

Some vendor items that should do well and complement your fair are:

- Jewelry
- Baskets
- Sheets and towels
- Kitchen gadgets and supplies
- Pet supplies
- New clothes, especially socks and accessories
- Baby items
- Leather goods
- Furniture
- Soap and perfume.

You might want to solicit nonprofit organizations to put up vendor booths, for example:

- Local ASPCA or animal shelter
- Volunteer firehouse
- Local museum for memberships
- Local charities

Offer these groups a special, lower nonprofit rate for the space. You might contact your local fraternal organizations, especially if they are sponsoring your fair, and give them a booth for free.

Where to find vendors? Usually when you have fairs with good attendance, vendors find you. But you can go out and solicit. Hawk other fairs and flea markets and pass out flyers about your own fair that state who's going to attend, how many people you're expecting, and the names and phone numbers of the PA volunteers who handle the vendor booths. Hand the flyer only to vendors whose wares are appropriate to your fair.

Run a small ad in a local newspaper classified section for vendors. Money from renting space to vendors is the easiest money you'll make at the fair, so give it a good push.

Designate a setup area for vendors. Draw a floor plan of all the space available for all the vendors. Plot out a special space for vendors that will get traffic, not someplace off to the side or out of the way. If the vendors don't sell anything, they won't be back next year. But on the other hand, if they make money, you can count on their coming back next year without having to solicit. So be helpful and give them good space.

Divide your vendor spot into ten- or twelve-foot spaces and number the spaces. Vendors who need more room can buy two spaces, perhaps for a discounted price. Draw or mark out the spaces and numbers on the ground in the area you've allocated to the vendors.

You can do this with chalk or neon-colored removable tape the day before the fair. Pull the tape off during cleanup after the fair.

Keep a written record of the spaces, numbers, and which vendors you've allocated to which spaces. Notify the vendors in advance, if you can, which space they have received. They can set up without trying to find you during the chaos before the fair. Don't place vendors selling similar merchandise next to one another.

NO-PARKING COMMITTEE

This is the thorniest responsibility of the fair. If cars are parked where you plan to have vendor booths, it will be a huge problem. If you are using actual city streets, then you will have cars parking there. You need to put up signs early in the week to alert drivers where there is no parking on the day of your fair. Put signs in the building lobbies on the street, asking tenants to please move their cars on the day of the fair.

Close the street off with police sawhorses or neon orange tape wound around garbage cans around midnight the night before. Closing the street early keeps from people from parking in the dark where they can't read the No Parking signs on the trees.

Put leaflets on the cars parked on the street. Getting the street cleared of all but two or three cars is a victory. Plan your vendor spaces with the idea that you may lose a few to people who refuse to move their cars. Have a few extra spaces tucked away, just in case.

PETTING ZOO

Locate a petting zoo through a local pet store, veterinarian, or the Internet. Try to get this attraction sponsored by a pet store or a local fraternal organization.

Block out a sizable area in the shade for your petting zoo. Find out from the owners how big the zoo is and how much space they need. Do not put the animals in the sun.

You need plenty of volunteers to guide the kids and fetch water for the animals and their trainers. A petting zoo is a big draw. If you have a sponsor, you can make a lot of money on a petting zoo. If you have to pay for it yourself, it may lose money or break even, because a petting zoo is expensive. But it will increase attendance significantly.

All the kids love a petting zoo. You need volunteers to make sure that the kids behave appropriately with the animals, so no one gets hurt. You need a clean-up crew at the end of the fair after the animals are gone. A petting zoo makes an ideal class booth for two or more upper-grade classes.

Remember to provide antibacterial hand wash or towelettes for the kids. Kids may go straight from the petting zoo to a food booth and need clean hands.

INSIDE EVENTS

Even if your event is on a beautiful day, schedule a few events inside the school auditorium to capitalize on the space. Since you may have to pay a fee for the custodians on Saturday anyway, why not use the school, too?

Put on a play or a puppet show during the fair. A talent show, where anyone can get up and sing, dance, make funny faces, do impressions, or stand-up comedy will work, too. How about a school band concert or a performance by a parent musician? A few inside events add to the fun and profit of your fair.

SECURITY

Security is terribly important. There's a lot of money floating around. Besides the ticket booth, which is fairly secure, there is money at all the food booths, the Secondhand Rose, secondhand clothes, books, and PA table, not to mention vendors. Have a plainclothes security team headed up by a board member. Any responsible person from the PA will do.

Even with a volunteer running security, hire men to be part of the security team. Gym teachers, school aides, even teachers make great security guards.

Retired or off-duty police make great security personnel. Hire a professional security team at $75 per day to augment parents and teachers.

Professional security guards get paid after the fair, when you have the funds readily available. Invest in a set of good, high-powered walkie-talkies for your security team. Have at least three roving security men assigned to a territory. You need security at each end of the fair and one or two people roaming through the crowds and checking in regularly at the booths that take in money.

Another part of the security job is to make sure the children are safe. If you close the street to traffic, the kids can run around on their own. Security people need to watch the crowds and make sure the children are safe.

You need security people inside the school. If your inside events occur on the first floor, security people need to keep everyone off the other floors to protect the school. You must keep the school open so people can use the bathrooms, even if there are no events going on inside the school. Once you open the school, you need security to keep vandals at bay. You also need to keep the school safe from thieves.

BANKING

Here is a banking system that works well if your treasurer and assistant treasurer are available to work the fair. Having two treasurers is a good idea as it spreads out the workload and keeps people honest. Every hour, the treasurer makes the rounds of each booth where the money, rather than tickets, changes hands.

At the booth, the treasurer counts the money earned that hour and takes most of it, leaving some for making change. The treasurer then gives a receipt to the person

who is working or in charge of that booth, stating the amount of money turned in and the time.

Hourly money pickup helps keep down risk of loss or theft. It is not good for the people handling the booths to have too much money at any time. This invites trouble. The person working the booth gives the receipt to the person in charge of the booth who can keep track of how much money was earned by adding up the receipts.

Only the treasurers should handle the money. Open up a classroom in the school and count money there. If you don't have a safe, perhaps you can convince the principal or other school official to lock the money in his or her desk or office.

Do not take money home from the fair. You can come back the following week and pick up the cash and deposit it, when no one will know how much money you have and it's safe to travel with the money. Back in the day, our fair netted over $30,000. The treasurers locked up the money and went home empty-handed at the end of the fair. That kept them safe.

Sell tickets good for the class booths, the maze, and the grab bags at a table in the middle of the big yard. Tickets may also be used for food and rides. This keeps most of the cash in one place, reducing the hassle of making change and cuts down on loss and theft.

PUBLICITY

Publicity is vital for any street fair. The street fair needs maximum attendance to make a good profit because the sums you take in are so small—a dollar here, two dollars here. You need to have as many people as possible pass through your fair to make the most of all the work everyone puts in and to generate a handsome return.

Create press kits with brightly colored folders containing flyers with all the pertinent information regarding the fair, such as time, place, and rain date which can be the following week. Include pictures of pervious fairs if you have them. If not, remember to take pictures of this fair so you can use them for the press kit next year. Include sheets with information about your school, the breakdown of the student body, and the activities the money will go to support. Put a black-and-white picture of your school on top of the sheets with school information.

If you have an art director in your parent body, recruit him or her to design flyers and information sheets so they look professional.

Send the press kits to the local newspapers, magazines, television, and radio stations. Write several thirty-second radio announcements and add them to the press kits going to the radio stations, who usually announce community events on the air.

Put up posters in local stores and shops. Send home notices in the backpacks of all the students in the school. Put it in your newsletter every week. Using a sheet and poster paint, create a huge banner to hung up on the school or on the school fence where passing cars can see it. Emphasize the time and date for the fair.

Put up small posters in the library, pediatricians' and other doctors' offices, dentists' offices, the hardware store, the fire station, the police station, the train station, the post office, the grocery store, and anywhere else you feel people who would come to the fair might be.

Send your press kits to the media at least two months in advance. Magazines should get the kits three months ahead, if possible.

CLEANUP AND MAKE A DONATION, AT THE SAME TIME

When the street fair is finished, there will be a surprising amount of left overs. Clothes, books, housewares, games, toys, and other white-elephant items will remain. It is a shame to throw this stuff out.

Call the Salvation Army or a thrift shop and alert them you'd like to donate all your leftover things if they will come and pick it up. What a relief! Any nonprofit organization, the ASPCA or local animal shelter, a homeless shelter, a church, any organization that needs clothes for people or has a secondhand shop can use your leftovers and will give them away or sell them to support their organization.

Call in advance and make arrangements. Double-check and make sure they are coming, confirm the time and location. This makes cleanup much easier.

AND DON'T FORGET...

Rent tables and chairs for your street fair. Even if you own some, you probably don't have enough. You need many long tables, one for each class booth, and several for other booths, not to mention offering a spot for people to sit and eat. The grab bags alone need three or four tables. And chairs are needed for every booth, too. It's easier to rent. They'll get delivered. When the fair's over, they pick them up. Chair and table rental is a necessary expense.

You also need a cleanup crew. This is the toughest job to fill. At the end of the fair, everyone is exhausted. Snag a few parents to knock down and pack up tables. Consider hiring a cleanup crew. Back in the day, we hired the Doe Foundation, a local organization that provided work for jobless and homeless men and women, to bring in people to make the schoolyard and street "broom clean." It's amazing to see that, an hour after the fair is over, it's as though it never happened. You must leave not only public areas but any common areas borrowed from your school in excellent condition.

JUST STARTING OUT?

If your parents association or school doesn't yet have funds for expenses, here is how you can start up your own street or school fair without a lot of money:

1. Use class booths that are not expensive, like the knock-down-the-milk cartons-with-a-tennis-ball, and others that only require inexpensive prizes that can be funded by parents' donations. Have as many class booths as possible. Class booths and a bake sale are the way my school started out.

2. Get as many small corporate sponsorship donations as you can. Even if a company only donates $50 or $100, it can be put together with other small donations to fund one ride, table-and-chair rental or something else you need.

3. Make 50 or 100 grab bags out of secondhand small toys donated by parents if you can't get new items donated.

4. A "store" to sell secondhand books, toys, and housewares doesn't require an outlay of money. Make these booths as big as possible. Price the merchandise low to sell as much as possible and generate more cash.

5. Have one or two massage chairs if you have parents who can do that in your school. Otherwise, approach professionals and ask if they would work the fair and split their proceeds with the school.

6. Have a school table. Create a modest raffle using secondhand bikes or donations of televisions, mixers, CD players, and such, in great condition.

7. Try for corporate donations to create a modest number of T-shirts, perhaps 50 or 100 to be sold at the fair.

8. Use a borrowed or donated small grill for hot dogs and hamburgers. Take up a collection to buy the food.

9. Skip the hot food and just have a bake sale at your first street or school fair. Get all baked good donated. Hopefully, they'll all be homemade; those sell best.

10. Skip the multicultural buffet unless you can get donated food and equipment. Perhaps one or two restaurants would like to sponsor tastings, where people pay a modest fee and receive tastings of several different kinds of food. This can be a good marketing tool for a restaurant, which will be responsible for bringing all utensils and plates.

11. You can still have music if you have a parent in the school willing to play for free. Music helps to attract and build crowds, which means more business for your fair.

12. Get one or two sponsors together to fund one $300 or $400 ride. One ride will be enough. You can add more rides each year as your attendance grows.

13. Have vendors. Vendors bring in money and don't' cost anything.

14. Make your flyers in the school, using the school copy machine to save money. Hand these out to vendors at other events. Inside events can still take place if the school produces them or someone volunteers to put on a show. Make the inside event a spelling bee, or a vocabulary or math competition. This creates excitement and doesn't cost anything, except for a modest prize.

15. Security is still mandatory. Try to get corporate sponsorship from a security company or at least a donation of one security man.

VOLUNTEERS

This event chews up more volunteers than any other event. You need probably 100 volunteers if you are producing a full-scale fair. If you're just starting out, you'll need fewer.

Here is a basic list:

1. Two overall chairs for the event
2. Committee chairs:

- Food (with the following subcommittee chairs: grill, bake sale, multicultural food)
- Class booths
- Rides
- Security
- Banking
- Publicity
- Corporate sponsorship
- Grab bags
- Secondhand clothes
- Books
- White elephant
- Vendors

- Cleanup
- School table
- Raffle
- Inside events
- Petting zoo
- The maze
- T-shirts

Each committee head will establish how many volunteers they need. You will need the majority of the school to get involved one way or another, even if it just means baking a pan of brownies or manning the class booth for an hour. The success of this event is composed of small contributions by a great many people. That's one of the secrets that makes this event such fun and creates a family feeling at the school. No one is left out of a street fair.

SECRETS TO SUCCESS

Grab bags are one of the secrets. Unusual class booths, great publicity, lots of parent participation, excellent food, and great rides all combine to make this fair a big success. Give a free T-shirt to every committee head and start T-shirt sales in school two weeks before the fair.

HOW MUCH MONEY WILL YOU RAISE?

The amount of money you take in depends upon several factors:

1. The weather—rain or the threat of rain will drive away customers.
2. The amount of publicity.
3. The amount of class participation in creating class booths.
4. School spirit

Back in the day, we raised more than $30,000 net after expenses. But we had a big school, and the Street Fair was a seasoned event. Smaller schools will raise less. But considering the amount of fun had by all, a street fair is always a hit.

TIMELINE

Because a fair takes so much time to plan, have it in the spring so you have plenty of time to plan and set up volunteers. Set a date a year ahead, if you can. The first Saturday after Memorial Day might be a good date, depending on where you live.

<u>As far in advance as possible</u>

Pick the date

File for your permits: if you need permission to close a street, serve liquor, or cook and serve food, get those permits filed in advance.

<u>Beginning of school year</u>

Apply for corporate sponsorships, begin vendor recruitment.

<u>Four months ahead</u>

Have a planning meeting with your committee heads to identify problems and brainstorm solutions.

Reserve rides. Gather raffles prizes.

<u>Three months ahead</u>

Line up all volunteers needed. Hire security people.

Find and hire petting zoo.

Select designs for T-shirts.

<u>Two/Three months ahead</u>

Get publicity out to all relevant media. Order T-shirts.

<u>Two months ahead</u>

Plan all food and make shopping lists.

Ask for grab bag donations from parents.

Send letters to companies asking for grab bag donations.

Have raffle tickets printed up.

<u>One month ahead</u>

Advertise in school newsletter for parent vendors.

Order additional grab bag items.

Assign vendor slots. Assign locations for class booths.

Gather materials for school table.

<u>Three weeks ahead</u>

Post sign-up sheets for donated food.

<u>Two weeks ahead</u>

Start publicity.

<u>One week ahead</u>

Make up grab bags.

Organize donations for secondhand books, clothes, and toys.

<u>Night before</u>

Assign locations for class booths.

Make the food that can be made in advance.

Put up "no parking" signs.

YEAR-ROUND EVENTS

The Flea Market

A small, enterprising group of parents came up with the idea for a flea market that has grown into a huge business supporting several schools today. They saw an opportunity to start it in the schoolyard of their children's middle school on Sundays. To be quite honest, the flea market was really started by vendors who snuck through a hole in the fence and set up shop. They were selling there for two years before parents noticed and decided to take over and start a real flea market.

Local residents resented the noise early on Sunday morning, the loss of parking spaces, and the mounting load of garbage that grew with the market. A greenmarket was added to the vendor mix, which helped to mollify residents, who quieted down since they bought beautiful fresh vegetables and fruit trucked in from the farm straight to their block. The farmer's market participation is key to winning over neighbors.

What started as a volunteer-run weekly event making a few dollars grew until it grossed $10,000 a month. Now under professional management, the flea market is a huge operation that makes several hundred thousand dollars per year. The rapid growth of the flea market meant it could no longer be run by volunteers. A professional manager and staff were hired to take over.

In the beginning, the parent volunteers carried tables, chairs, and other paraphernalia out to the schoolyard. They collected fees from the vendors, counted the money, did the bookkeeping, and administered all the paperwork. At the end of the day, they carried the tables and chairs back into the school building, swept, and collected the garbage.

Obviously, this was too much work for parent volunteers alone. They needed to hire a manager. Even so, they needed parent volunteers. They couldn't count on a steady or consistent bunch of parents, so they hired employees. Still, all the bookkeeping, legal, and administrative functions were done by parent volunteers.

It's wonderful that the money being raised does not come out of the pockets of the parents. The flea market thrives on neighborhood traffic and buyers who come from all over the city.

The fund-raiser can make more money than all the other fund-raisers combined. But it'll grow so big it will need to be professionally run. Be sure to consult an accountant and an attorney when you start setting up your school flea market.

Why? The money from the flea market that flowed into the parents association, which was considerable, would be considered nonrelated business income and would therefore be subject to federal, state, and local business income taxes. That would put a serious dent in the profits from all that hard work and ingenuity.

On the advice of tax counsel, the parents had a for-profit corporation known as Green Flea, Inc. created to operate the flea market in order to protect the tax-free transfer of money from the market operations to the parents associations. The creation of Green Flea Corporation allowed money to be paid tax-free to the school PA as a royalty.

This will all be much less complicated if you have only one school involved in your flea market. But you may wish to pull your district schools together to create and run a central flea market, or you may benefit from joining up with one other school. You'll have to share profits, but you'll also have a much larger pool of volunteers to draw from. Here is how you start a flea market of your own.

WHAT IS A FLEA MARKET?

A flea market is a group of people selling goods—from jewelry to fresh vegetables—to the general public set up in an area like a big schoolyard or parking lot. Frequently the vendors offer lower-priced merchandise than traditional retail establishments since they are not paying rent each week but only a small fee to the owner or operator of the flea market space.

HOW DO YOU SET UP A FLEA MARKET?

First you have to have a schoolyard or parking lot as well as some space inside the school, like a hallway and the cafeteria, to expand your market and to use for bad weather. School bathrooms need to be available.

The school needs a great location where it will draw shoppers from across the community, not just the parents from the school. A flea market cannot survive week after week with only parent buyers. Just as in any real estate transaction, location is everything. A flea market does not cost much to start, so it's ideal for a school just beginning a fundraising program.

Think of your flea market as a new mall being constructed. Would there be enough shopper traffic in the neighborhood? Is the school located near downtown? Is it in a neighborhood with lots of people doing errands and out on the streets on the day you will run the market? If the answer to these questions is no, don't give up. Perhaps you don't have enough traffic to run a flea market fifty-two weeks a year, but how about two or four times a year?

How about only before holidays? Could you run a flea market in November and December for holiday shoppers and again in April and May before Mother's

Day and Father's Day? Think creatively and be flexible and open to the ideas of others.

Not sure if a flea market could be successful at your school? Test it out. It doesn't require much of an investment other than time to try it out. To test a market and get an accurate reading on whether or not a flea market will work, you must run for at least five or six weeks in a row, maybe longer. One or two weeks will not give you enough information to decide whether your flea market will be a success. What if you have rain or snow for one or two weekends? You also have to allow enough time for the word to get out that the flea market is there and that the merchandise is good.

Take time to figure out what will work best for your school. Be honest about the retail potential of the site. If it isn't good, consider testing a smaller format: fewer vendors, three times per year.

If you are successful, hire a manager. Remember, parent volunteers are not only hard to come by, but when their children graduate from the school, they move on, taking their knowledge and experience with them. If you hire a good manager, he or she will be there year in and year out.

Find out from your principal who you have to contact to get permission to use the school on weekends. Is there a permit fee to cover the time-and-a-half salary of the custodian who must be there to open the school, clean up after the market, and close the school.

Draw a map of the total area available to you and carve it up into separate spaces. Assign rental cost to each space based on its size and location. Or offer the spaces as singles or two spaces together as doubles, which may be more appealing for vendors who need larger spaces, like farmers. Each vendor pays rent for space. That money goes to the flea market.

Why doesn't the flea market take a percentage of the vendor's sales? Wouldn't they make more money that way? Not necessarily. There are several compelling reasons why a good flea market doesn't provide space on a percentage basis:

1. It would be impossible to document what was sold and how much money the vendor made from sales each day.
2. Would you take your percentage on the gross sales or net, (sales less the cost of goods and expenses)? How would you determine the net for all the items sold?
3. Giving space on a percentage-of-sales basis means the flea market would be making an investment in the vendor, or rolling the dice, taking the chance the vendor has the right goods, displayed well, and priced right for sale. Taking that

kind of chance without having any control over the items sold and the price could be a disaster.

There are simply too many variables to keep track of. The book-keeping would be a nightmare and would have to be done at the end of each day before the vendor leaves so you can collect your share. This would be impossible if you have five vendors or more.

1. The flea market would be hurt if the weather turned bad or the flow of buyers went down for a week.

Instead of accepting any risk with the vendors, a well-run flea market just charges a flat fee, depending upon the size of the space. Make the fee reasonable to keep the market profitable so vendors return to the market to sell every week. The flea market makes its money on vendors who come week after week.

Give a discount to vendors for repeat business. Make special offers, like rent for three consecutive weeks and get the fourth week free. This is good if you are just starting out. Even if you're not, if there is space left that you're not collecting money for, you do better to make a few dollars on that space than to make nothing.

Try a standby offer for parents in the school. If they come for a last-minute space, they only pay half the rental fee—if there is space available.

Be creative and keep testing offers to see which ones bring in the most response from vendors. Be careful not to stress the remaindered space because you may have vendors who pull out and just wait for re-maindered space, thus leaving you to sell too much space at half price.

Be careful about raising the rent for space. You need to keep new vendors coming in. If the rates get too high, you may be bringing in the wrong type of vendors, ones selling merchandise that is too high priced for your crowd of shoppers. Antique and craft vendors will draw more crowds and more repeat customers than displays of new merchandise or gimmicky gadgets.

Low rents allow for vendor consistency. Having the same vendors every week matters to shoppers. I get all my family's athletic socks and apples from the vendors at our flea market.

I don't want to come back and find that when we need socks, the vendor isn't there. My children mourned when the little china-animal lady retired and they could no longer visit her table, studying the new tiny china creatures and begging me to buy one.

Vendors complain if you're charging too much for space. It is more important to have a high occupancy percentage than it is to take in the maximum on each rental. Aim for an occupancy rate of over 65 percent each week. Steady rental customers are the best way to make money. Don't be greedy by trying to get the highest price possible for vendor space. You may find yourself with an empty flea market.

Consider using peak and off-peak season pricing. Also, any vendor who rents 34 times per year pays the lowest average rent. Only the people renting in the best seasons—usually holidays, spring, and fall—pay more.

Give space free or at half the rent for community organizations such as the Girl and Boy Scouts, ASPCA, dog and cat rescue groups, not-for-profit theater groups, soup kitchens, and other organizations that are trying to raise money for the homeless. This will bring you both goodwill in the community and a whole new group of shoppers.

- Reserve a table for the PA. Have a bake or a white elephant sale.

ORGANIZATION

A successful flea market can grow quickly and become too big to be run by volunteers. But before you grow, you have to start out with volunteer power. Here is a list of weekly tasks. Divide them up to work efficiently.

- By Wednesday, you will be receiving calls from vendors to reserve space. Use an answering machine to take vendor reservations.
- Create a chart and/or drawing of the space that you can write on each week so you can keep track of who's renting which space. You may want to start out on a first-come, first-served basis on space until you have a steady stream of reliable vendors. Renting on a first-come basis may be difficult for vendors as people start lining up at 6:00 a.m. to get a spot.
  - But until you know who is reliable, this is the best method of renting out space. Then you will not be sitting with unsold space because someone reserved space and didn't show. You may have turned down someone reliable because you erroneously thought you were sold out, which means lost revenue.
  - Keep track of every vendor and collect cash the day of the flea market for the space. Do not accept checks or money orders. Too many checks bounce. Thieves or con men may rip you off, passing you bad checks. Credit cards make it much easier and safer. You need at least two people to collect and count the cash to keep everything honest and make sure that no cash disappears.
- Use strict guidelines on handling money. Your manager should be responsible to ensure that there is no payroll padding, like paying one person twice for the same job. You

need an experienced bookkeeper or accountant to help you set up the finances correctly and put safeguards in place. Put out the word among the parents in your school in your search for professional help.

- You need liability insurance no matter the size of your flea market. If someone gets injured, your market can be wiped out financially if you don't have insurance. Insurance is based on the size of your business. Try to find a reputable insurance broker in your parent body. Keep excellent records and show up for your insurance audit. Our manager saved $20,000 in insurance payments just by going to the audit and finding an error. If you have employees, you will need workmen's compensation insurance, in addition to liability insurance.

- Hire an experienced manager. Your flea market is not a place to learn on the job. Get a manager who can hit the ground running and get your flea market up and bringing in revenue quickly, efficiently, and correctly.

- Advertise to bring buyers to the flea market. Start with your school newsletter—it's free.

- In the beginning, you may need to advertise to attract vendors. After you have been up and running for a while, vendors will find out about your market from word of mouth.

TIP: *Offer vendor slots at a very low rate first to the parents in your school. You never know who does crafts they'd like to sell or wants to set* up a *lemonade and homemade cookie stand. Make the same discounted space offer to teachers.*

- You need an advertising budget. Advertise where you will reach the most people. Place ads in newspapers near the garage sale pages. Many garage sale addicts love flea markets, too. Advertising can also include signs in the local supermarket and hardware store windows. Put up posters at school and houses of worship. It is important to attract as many buyers as possible. Don't overlook neighboring towns for advertising. When you have a big crowd of buyers, vendors will seek out your flea market, and you'll be in business.

TIP: Remember those large folding tables and chairs? Rent them to vendors who don't have tables. Offer chair and table rental inexpensively. It's extra revenue. Table rental service makes it much easier for beginners to become vendors at our market. Table and chair rental income adds up quickly.

DON'T FORGET

- You need the custodian. Be nice to him, address him courteously. Treat him with respect. Give him a gift or card at holiday time and remember his birthday.
- You need permission from the principal of the school where you are holding the flea market. Maybe the school superintendent as well.
  - Only start a flea market if your school space gets lots of traffic from people other than the parents at the school—for example, if your school is on a street that leads to a supermarket, movie theater, mall, or house of worship. If your school doesn't get that much outside traffic, consider running a flea market on a more limited basis, either quarterly or only during holiday times, like Christmas and Mother's Day.
- Provide both outdoor and indoor space. Outdoor space usually works best as people can see the tables and the goods, but indoor space is extra space and may be key during bad weather.
- Get local farmers to bring in fruits and vegetables. It draws people from all over to buy the produce trucked in so fresh the

grocery stores can't compete.

- Hire staff to double as both security guards and cleanup crew. You need at least two people—maybe more, depending on the size of your flea market.
- Track monthly payments to vendors and keep excellent records for the state. Special income-and-expense-reporting requirements may be imposed on your flea market by your state.
- Start a vendor hotline and take reservations on Monday and Tuesday.
- On Wednesday, call each vendor to give them their assigned space for the market. A lottery for space on Saturday or Sunday morning may reduce the number of vendors. You might have long lines and run out of space, creating angry vendors, which is not good for business. Back in the day, the first-come, first-served method didn't work for our school since early arrivals tended to be vendors selling junky merchandise.
- The most successful flea markets keep some control over the type of merchandise sold. Don't allow just anyone who has money to come; be choosy, picking which vendors you sell space to. In the long run, it improves your profits and builds a solid reputation among buyers, confident they can find good merchandise at your flea *market*.

TIP: Leave the area you are using spotless. You will lose permission to use the space if there is garbage piled up on Monday morning. Don't rely on the school custodian to take care of cleanup. If he doesn't do a good job, it reflects badly on your operation.

PRICING

Price space rental very low to begin with. Get a consensus from your board members about how much to charge. Starting at $25 or $30 might work. It depends on your location and population. You can always raise your rates as the market grows. But if you're priced too high, vendors won't make enough money to come back again. As you grow, assign prices by location. Outside space might cost more than indoor, for example.

TIP: Special offers are good, especially when you are starting out.

The most important goal is to have all the spaces rented, even if the rates are low. This way you make the most money and are able to pay your staff, keep going, and build a reputation. As the market gets established and you have regular shoppers, you can raise the space rental rates and vendors will gladly pay the higher prices if they are consistently selling merchandise and making money.

The Ultimate Bake Sale

THE IN-SCHOOL BAKE SALE

An in-school bake sale takes place before, during, and after school. The buyers are parents, teachers, and the students. Here are some tips to make the in-school bake sale a success.

- Kids buy store-bought baked good that adults will not. For example, Entenmann's chocolate-chip cookies, priced at two for 50¢, will sell to kids at the in-school bake sale, but not out-of-school sales that appeal mostly to adults.

- Besides baked goods, candy, chips, pretzels, other snacks, soda, and water may sell well. Send parents to the nearest discount store or warehouse club to buy huge containers of individually wrapped candy, like Twizzlers, and sell them for two for 50¢. Inexpensive items allow everyone at the school to buy something at without it being a big expense. Full participation is good not only for the morale and self-esteem of the children, but it generates income and good feelings, too.

- Make sure you have plenty to sell. Running out of merchandise kills a bake sale fast. Send a volunteer to buy more to sell when donations get low and you'll generate income all day long.

- Start the sale early, about half an hour before school starts. You'll reach early parent and teacher arrivals.

- Sell bagels with butter or cream cheese to the early birds.

- Place your sale strategically to reach the most people. Use the lobby where many students and teachers pass on the way to the classrooms in the morning.

- Arrange for teachers to bring their classes down to the bake sale, one class at a time. Post a sign-up sheet on the office door for teachers to pick a time to bring their class down for ten minutes or so for the kids to buy goodies.

- Publicize the bake sale not only to those from whom you are requesting donations but also to everyone in the school, so every kid can bring money. Most younger children don't carry money to school, so you need to remind them to bring $1 for the sale.
- Charge lower prices than you would for an out-of-school bake sale.
- If a child doesn't have enough money, sell the item to them for whatever they have. If they don't have any money, let them select something small to take with them for free.
- Be sure to get the word out to all the parents. You need two parents per hour to help run the table. The same parents can cover several hours. Everyone should make some contribution. Those who can't work the table can bake something. Promote your goal—how you plan to spend the proceeds. Parents are more likely to contribute when they know where the money is going.
- There are several ways to safely handle bake sale cash. Deposit the cash in the school safe frequently. I don't like to keep more than about $50 in change and low-denomination bills with me at the bake sale. If you don't have a safe, you can send two reliable parents to the bank several times during the day. Store cash that comes in after banking hours in the principal's office. Prevent loss and theft.

ELECTION DAY BAKE SALE

Have sales directed to non-school adults and children a few times a year, depending upon local events. Since all the voting in NYC usually takes place in schools, Primary and Regular Election Day bake sales happen all over the Big Apple. If your school is also a voting place, you're guaranteed a large group of adult buyers traipsing by your tables.

TIP: If the voting place is not in your school, get permission to hold a bake sale wherever people go to vote. This is a crucial time to raise money from members of your community, not just your parents.

Here are some do's and don'ts for Election Day bake sales in your school.

- Set up early. Try to get the table up and running before 8:00 a.m. since many people vote before going to work. If you start setting up at 6:30, you'll be ready by 7:30 when people start arriving.
- Sell coffee, especially in the morning. Invest in an electric coffeepot that makes 50 to 100 cups. Get it up and perking early as it takes half an hour to forty-five minutes to make the coffee. Coffee sells well, especially to people who won't buy baked goods because of dietary restrictions. Sell the coffee for $2 a cup. That's a whole lot less than Starbucks.

TIP: Try to get coffee donated from Starbucks, a local coffee roaster, or supermarket in exchange for promoting where the coffee came from. This will increase sales. Otherwise, go to a discount store where you can get a gigantic can of coffee for the best price.

- Sell only homemade bakes goods. The biggest question an Election Day bake sale is: "What's homemade?" Even if your prices are higher than those at the in-school bake sale, they are still lower than a bakery's prices. People love to buy homemade baked goods.
- One exception to store-bought goods is Krispy Kreme donuts. Everyone loves these doughnuts and will buy them no matter what. Krispy Kreme promotes fund-raising. Here's their website:
- https://krispykreme.com/fund-raising/home Back in the day, they donated donuts on Election Day. Ask, the most they can

do is say "no."

- In the evening, continue to sell coffee, but add cold soda and water, which will sell well with and adult crowd, too, especially with people watching their calories and cholesterol. Everyone can buy a bottle water for a buck and feel like a contributor to your school. Water and soda should be bought at a discount store or a beverage outlet. Borrow a giant garbage can from a custodian, line it with a triple layer of thick garbage bags, fill it with ice, and add the drinks. Profits from drinks add up quickly.

- Concentrate your selling during peak hours: 7:00 to 11:00 a.m. and 3:00 to 8:00 p.m. If there's not much traffic, it wastes volunteers to man the table if there are almost no sales to be made. Pack things up loosely and stow them under the table so you can open up again quickly after lunch.

- Presentation is important, especially for the out-of-school bake sale. Use tablecloths, attractive serving platters, paper napkins, and paper plates.

- Whole cakes are best in the out-of-school bake sale. You might be able to sell a whole cake. But even if you don't, cakes generate a good profit. If you slice a cake up into ten pieces, and sell each one at $3, you will raise $30 from each cake donated.

There are a greater variety of cakes than cupcakes, where decorations usually take the cake! Homemade angel food cakes have always been one of our top sellers. But you can have lemon cakes, Bundt cakes, coconut cakes, pound cakes, and of course chocolate cakes.

If you sell cakes, don't forget plastic forks. Ask for donations of paper goods and plastic utensils from parents who don't have time to bake anything.

- Pie works great by the slice or by the whole pie. Sweet potato pie is a favorite.

- In the morning, sell bagels with cream cheese or butter with coffee. These are perfect items for parents who can't bake to donate. Bagels sell well to people who don't want to make another stop on their way to work. Sell homemade muffins in the morning. Corn or blueberry do well, or throw in mini chocolate chips and make chocolate chip corn muffins, a big seller. Any breakfast pastry is also a surefire hit.

- Use kids to help sell. On major election days, when school is out, running a bake sale table gives the kids something positive and fun to do with their time. Adults respond well to the children at the table, and their presence makes your customers feel more connected to the school. Adults like to see children working for things instead of just expecting handouts.

- Try homemade sandwiches during lunchtime at an Election Day bake sale. A voter stuck in a long line eating up lunch hour is a captive customer for a convenient and well-priced premade sandwich.

TIP: Back in the day, bananas were a big hit in our high school Election Day bake sale. People who were more health-conscious preferred the fruit. We charge a dollar for one and didn't get many complaints.

SPECIAL-OCCASION BAKE SALE

- Every community has special events that bring people out in droves. Memorial Day Parade? Easter Parade? Town celebration? Plan a bake sale to coincide with a special event.

- How about a made-to-order pumpkin pie sale with delivery the day before Thanksgiving? Would parents in your school prefer to pre-order a pie than bake it themselves? Would parents in your school be willing to bake-to-order?

SECRETS TO SUCCESS

For the in-school bake sale: buy big containers of giant pretzel sticks or small individual boxes or pretzels, and boxes of individually packaged cookies at a discount store and sell the individual packages for a buck.

When you get low on baked goods, pretzels, chips, or whatever you're selling, go out and buy more, such as bags of cookies or a box of doughnuts, from a local store with the money you're making on the sale. This keeps you in supplies all day and helps to cover the bare spots when supplies get low.

Election Day or special-occasion bake sale: add a donation jar to your table. People who don't want to buy baked goods may still want to contribute to your school. You'd be surprised how much money you can make from simple dollar and five-dollar donations.

Advertise your purpose for the sale. Back in the day, at an Election Day bake sale, we received donations of $5, $10, and $20 when we told people we were raising money to pay for paraprofessionals in kindergarten classrooms.

TIP: Have a themed bake sale—a pumpkin/mince pie and cranberry bread bake sale right before Thanksgiving. A Christmas cookie bake sale before the holiday is a festive fund-raiser.

VOLUNTEERS

At out-of-school sales, have children join their parents at the bake sale table. This gives the kids a chance to practice math and learn to make change. They feel like part of the process.

You need two kinds of volunteers: parents who supply you with baked goods to sell, and parents who man the table. Two volunteers works best since there is much to do with wrapping the purchases "to go," getting forks, and counting out change.

HOW MUCH MONEY WILL YOU RAISE?

The amount of money you raise depends on how many baked goods, cups of coffee, tea, and other items for sale you have. Also, include the income from your donation jar.

It's possible to make over a thousand dollars from a well-run bake sale, with mouth-watering food in a high traffic area. It's amazing how fast those one-and-two-dollar-purchases add up.

TIMELINE

This event can be thrown together in a week if you do the right publicity and have a good group of parents who will bake, but three weeks ahead is a preferable time frame. If you have a bake sale every year at the same time—like an Election Day bake sale—then start the publicity early to remind people.

<u>Three weeks ahead</u>
Start publicity.
Start soliciting donations.
Send home sign-up sheets and flyers by backpack or on email.

<u>Two weeks ahead</u>
Reserve tables with the custodian.
Email reminders to parents.
Publish in school newsletter. Put up posters.

<u>One week ahead</u>
Solicit donations from bakeries and doughnut shops.
Remind parents to bake.
Shop at discount stores and beverage wholesalers.
Put reminder in newsletter.

<u>Day before</u>
Arrange for extension cords, etc. for coffee machines.
Arrange for ice and garbage cans.
Gather paper goods donations.

Candy Sales

WHAT IS A CANDY SALE?

There are different kinds of candy sales, run through a variety of candy companies. The school buys boxes of candy bars, sells them to the public for $1 per bar, netting a 50 percent profit.

HOW DOES A CANDY SALE WORK?

Your school either circulates a catalog of candy products or orders the candy direct and then sells it. You should make a profit of 50 percent from candy sales. Anything less may not be worth the effort. Most candy sales are done in the fall, when people are most enthusiastic and not burned-out from fund-raising.

Find a company that is set up to do candy sales. Here are a few to explore:

- World's Finest Chocolate Company. They are primarily a fund-raising company. I haven't used them, so I can't vouch for their claims. But they appear to be experienced and have simplified the process of ordering and selling chocolate. They require a minimum purchase of eight cases of candy bars. Check them out here:
- https://worldsfinestchocolate.com/start-fund-raising/get-started[1] (chocolate)
- www.allstarfund-raising.net[2] (chocolate and popcorn)
- www.ezfund.com[3] (pretzel rods and cookie dough)
- www.fivestarfund-raising.com[4] (cookie dough, popcorn, candy bars)
- https://www.promotioninmotion.com/fund-raising/   (kid's

---

1. https://worldsfinestchocolate.com/start-fundraising/get-started

2. http://www.allstarfundraising.net

3. http://www.ezfund.com

4. http://www.fivestarfundraising.com

favorite candy)
- www.thechippery.com[5] (cookie dough)

TIP: Cookie dough sales are popular. After buying a tub of cookie dough, I understand why. Imagine being able to bake half a dozen or a dozen cookies in a heartbeat? Yes, just scoop the dough and bake to get fresh warm-from-the-oven cookies! Because you keep the dough in the freezer, you can make as many or as few as you wish. If candy sales don't appeal to you, try this instead.

SECRETS OF SUCCESS

in offices to boost sales. A box of chocolate bars is a great reward at the office. Or have parents take a box or two to the office and sell them.

VOLUNTEERS

Another nice part of this fund-raiser is that it doesn't chew up a lot of volunteers. You only need about three people to have a candy sale fund-raiser.

HOW MUCH MONEY WILL YOU RAISE?

This depends on the size of your school. This is a fund-raiser you can start small and build.

TIMELINE

Two Months Ahead

Decide on the company you want to use and type of plan you want.

One Month Ahead

Order the candy.

Start your publicity.

CAVEAT: This fund-raiser works particularly well when the kids sell the candy. Do not, under any circumstances, send your children out to sell candy by themselves. If you want them to sell it, they must be accompanied by an adult. No door-to-door sales without a grown-up along.

NOTE: I'm not a fan of using product sales alone to raise money for the PA. My experience has been with events that create a sense of community, a strong bond among parents, teachers, the administration, and the students. Fund-raising can do more than simply raise money, it connects a child to their school in a positive way.

I have included candy and other food product sales here because it's a quick and easy fund-raiser. It's one that is known to most people.

The School Store

WHAT IS A SCHOOL STORE?

The school store is an area in the school designated solely for selling merchandise displaying the school logo and colors.

HOW DOES A SCHOOL STORE WORK?

The school store can make money all year long if you have enough people to run it and reorder supplies. Try opening once or twice a month, or once a week at first. If you have enough volunteers and the store is making money, increase the number of days the store is open.

You need capital to start the store since you have to buy items and pay for them before you sell. Items for the store can be ordered from a company that personalizes products, offers the lowest price, and the best service.

Some items up might sell in the school store include:

- Pens, pencils, funky erasers
- Book covers or protectors
- Notebooks, binders
- Backpacks, flashlights, umbrellas
- Mugs, key chains
- Sweatshirts, T-shirts, ball caps, sweat shirts.

Some online companies that provide personalized products are:

- www.customprinting.com[6]
- www.discountmugs.com[7]
- www.epromos.com[8]
- www.iprint.com[9]

---

6. http://www.customprinting.com

7. http://www.discountmugs.com

8. http://www.epromos.com

- www.logo-it.com[10]
- www.thediscountprinter.com[11]
- www.vistaprint.com[12]

CAVEAT: I only have personal experience with Discount Mugs and Vistaprint. Both companies gave good prices and service.

VOLUNTEERS

You need several volunteers to man the store on the day(s) you are open. Have two volunteers for each shift. If your store is very small, one will do, but it's always better to have two people handling cash. You need a committee head who orders products and keeps the books to track expenses and income. Create your own catalog and price list and distribute to everyone through email.

SECRETS TO SUCCESS

Have a table selling imprinted items at the school fair and parent/teacher conferences. Add some logo items to an in-school bake sale. List items and prices on a special page in your newsletter the week the store is open. Set up your store on a big cart you can keep in a school closet.

Pull it out for sporting events, bake sales, book fairs, and conferences. Publicity is important. Parents need to know when the store is going to be open. Post the hours around the school, put in your newsletter, and send in an email to all the parents.

HOW MUCH MONEY WILL YOU RAISE?

This depends upon how much you invest and how long it takes to sell the items. Mark up items by at least 50% to make a profit. Mark up the less expensive items 100%. If a logo pen costs $0.75 cents to buy, sell it for $1.50. T-shirts with a beautiful logo design can bring in well over

9. http://www.iprint.com

10. http://www.logo-it.com

11. http://www.thediscountprinter.com

12. http://www.vistaprint.com

a thousand dollars. Of course, this depends on the size of your school. This is a business you can grow slowly and profitably.

TIMELINE

Have your designs ready by September. The earlier you order merchandise, the sooner you can begin selling.

JUST STARTING OUT?

You need money to start a school store, but you can start small. Even just $100 collected from parents $5 at a time can get you started. Try to find a corporate sponsor to kick in $200 to $500 to start your store.

Negotiate with your suppliers for a lower price or extra merchandise. Get prices from competing companies and play them off each other until you get a price you can afford.

Pencils might be the best place to start as you can buy them so cheaply—$0.30 a piece for a gross (144 pencils) at www.penfactory.com[13]. This is imprinting only with your school's name—not a logo. But that costs less than $50.00 for 144. Sell them for $0.60 each and make 100% profit.

Try:

- www.4imprint.com[14]
- https://www.usschoolsupply.com/
- www.orientaltrading.com[15]

Reinvest your profit by buying more products and your business should flourish.

---

13.   http://www.penfactory.com

14. http://www.4imprint.com

15. http://www.orientaltrading.com

TAPPING CORPORATE AMERICA

With money for schools getting harder and harder to find, more parents are turning to the corporate world for help. Smart marketing people are finding many different ways to encourage purchase or trial of their company's products by reaching out to schools.

These companies are willing to reserve a small amount of the profits as a donation to those schools. Following are some companies with excellent school fund-raising promotions that are easy to bring to your school.

Adopt-A-Classroom

Adopt-A-Classroom one of the leading educational charities in the country, is a nonprofit organization that harnesses the resources of the community, major corporations, and the Internet to support educational experiences for students. https://www.adoptaclassroom.org/

Adopt-A-Classroom has been around for 21 years. They have helped over 200,000 classrooms get the supplies they need. They have supported 4.5 million students and raised $36 million!

Jamie Rosenberg, the founder of Adopt-A-Classroom, is a lawyer who saw teachers reaching into their own pockets for classroom supplies and started this remarkable organization. He realized the gap between paltry school budgets and the need for classroom supplies.

Rosenberg found individuals, organizations, and businesses willing to sponsor classrooms with donations. Rosenberg then gave up his corporate life to run Adopt-A-Classroom, a program benefiting schools.

HOW ADOPT-A-CLASSROOM WORKS

Adopt-A-Classroom connects sponsors and donors to teachers and schools locally, nationally, and by area of interest. They help K-12 teachers and principals in public, private, and charter schools in any community across the U.S., including all U.S. territories.

They make it easy for teachers and schools to register, receive funds, and order the supplies they want and need.

Teachers spend an average of $740 a year of their own money on classroom supplies. Since 1998, Adopt-A-Classroom has connected donors to teachers with grants, sponsorship, and crowdfunding. New in 2019, Adopt-A-Classroom's fund-raising platform is now available to public, private, and charter schools across the country. Not just classrooms, but schools are now eligible for their grants and sponsorship funding.

To be eligible to receive Adopt-A-Classroom supplies free, a teacher must apply directly online. Principal approval is also required. A school may apply, too, but district approval is required.

The teacher and/or the school creates a fund-raising page, describing their needs. Once the page has gone public, donations may come from the school's community, parents, local businesses, or Adopt-A-Classroom partners.

While you may love their program, Adopt-A-Classroom will only deal with teachers and school administrators, not parents or parents associations. Publicize this wonderful organization to all the teachers in your school and the principal.

The teachers and principal must go to www.adoptaclassroom.com[1], to apply for the stipend. There are step-by-step instructions for teachers and administrators. Urge your teachers to register!

Box Tops 4 Education

WHAT IS BOX TOPS 4 EDUCATION?

This is a fund-raising program run by General Mills. In the past, parents, friends, and family would have to gather labels of qualifying products. Not anymore! Box Tops is changing to fit today's families. The new-and-improved Box Tops mobile app uses state-of-the-art technology to scan your store receipt, find participating products, and instantly add Box Tops to your school's earnings online. Download it from the App Store or get it on Google Play.

Eventually, this program will be all digital. Go to www.boxtops4education.com[2] to learn how the labels will change and how the program works. Each label you scan will earn ten cents ($0.10) for your school. That doesn't sound like a lot of money, but it adds up. If all parents in the school scan in their grocery labels and buy products with the Box Tops 4 Education logo, you'll be surprised how much money to come to your school.

New in 2019, their fund-raising platform is now available to public, private, and charter schools across the country. Schools are also eligible for our grants and sponsorship funding.

Since 1997, Box Tops has generated $913,710,018 and counting! The list of participating products is huge. Check their website to see all the products in this program. https://www.boxtops4education.com/Participating-Products-Page

HOW THE PLAN WORKS

1. Buy General Mills products from the list on the above website.
2. Save the Box Tops 4 Education logo by cutting it off the top of the box. Or scan your receipt with the app.
3. Turn the box tops in to your school coordinator.
4. Count and bundle the box tops and send them to General

2.   http://www.boxtops4education.com

Mills by the deadline.

5. General Mills will send you a check! The box tops are worth 10¢ each. But when you have hundreds of people saving box tops over time, it adds up. Raise hundreds of dollars or even thousands, to spend any way the school pleases.

Register your school at www.boxtops4education.com[3] and get started today.

TIP: *Check the Box Tops website regularly for special offers. They have occasional sweepstakes and special offer for Costco and other big box stores.*

---

3.   http://www.boxtops4education.com

Retail On-Site Fund-Raising Events

Every year at Christmas, I buy books as gifts and have them wrapped by parents from a school or people from a nonprofit wrapping packages for a donation. If you don't have a Barnes & Noble near you, is there a gift shop that would allow you to wrap for them and collect a donation from the buyer?

Get volunteers to take over shifts. Three volunteers for one hour periods should be enough. Don't forget to thank the store and publicize it in your school community. If parents buy from that store, the proprietor will be more amenable to continuing the relationship with your school

FAST FOOD

Burger King, McDonald's, and Pizza Hut have programs open to schools, Scouts, and other nonprofit organizations. Create your night at Burger King. Call around to the local franchises of national food chains and present this innovative idea to the owner or manager.

HOW IT WORKS

The fast-food restaurant agrees to give a percentage of the gross from receipts collected at a specific time, on a particular night—for example, from 3p.m. to 5p.m. on a Wednesday.

Use publicity to get as many parents and caregivers to show up with their kids. The whole evening felt like a school or class potluck with no one cooking and no one cleaning up. You might make only a few hundred dollars, but it's very easy and the money is pure profit.

Go into any store or restaurant in your community—especially those known to be popular with your students—and arrange to have a special night there for your school. Let the restaurant or store pick and especially slow night so you can increase their traffic and total receipts. This opportunity to join hands with retail establishment to increase their sales while making money for your school is a win/win. Joining fun with fund-raising is an unbeatable combination.

HIGH SCHOOL FUND-RAISING

High school needs are different than lower schools. Thus the fund-raising, though still necessary, must be carried out differently. High school students come and go on their own. There will be no backpacks to stuff flyers or newsletters into.

Students on teams will raise their own funds to support their teams. Candy sales are popular for this. High school classes are conducted by subject. The student doesn't remain in one classroom with one teacher all day. There will be no class parents, no events conducted for students like the PA did in the lower schools.

GOALS

In high school, the PA should focus on supporting the parents and the principal. Parents may face their biggest challenges as their children enter teenage years. With more autonomy and independence may come more exposure to drugs. And rebellion, often necessary for teens to stand on their own, makes for a difficult time for parents.

HELPING PARENTS

The PA can help parents by having the funds to hire experts to conduct seminars or talks on coping with teenagers and preparing for college. At Brooklyn Technical High School, where I was on the PA Board, the PA paid for the woman who wrote the book *The Colleges that Change Lives* to speak at our school.

TIP: We paid for someone to speak to the parents about how to fill out the FAFSA form to apply for a federal
scholarship to college for their child. https://studentaid.ed.gov/sa/fafsa

We invited all the college admission test preparation companies to come to a PA meeting and distribute their materials to our parents.

HELPING THE PRINCIPAL

The PA should establish a principal's discretionary fund. There will be needs the school and the principal will have that cannot be taken care of by his or her district. For example, Brooklyn Tech had two finalists for the National Chess Championship tournament who needed to fly to Arizona to compete but didn't have the money for the airline ticket. The principal approached the PA, and we bought the tickets.

Working through the principal, the parents of high school students can make funds available for specialized classroom equipment, sports equipment, musical instruments, props for a school play, or to pay for entertainment, like a play or an opera to be performed at the school, that is not covered by the district.

At Tech, we bought a secondhand van for our principal to use to transport the football team to away games.

The needs of a high school principal are different than those of lower schools. He or she needs the PA to stand behind him or her and help fill those needs.

ACHIEVING THOSE GOALS

Most methods of school fund-raising discussed earlier in this book won't apply to high school fund-raising. Here are the best ways to raise money from high school parents:

- Pledge drive. Sending a pledge drive letter

in the first week of school to your parents, outlining how you plan to spend the money, is key. Email the letter or let the school either email it for you or print and mail it for you. Knowing how much this will help your principal, he or she should be willing to help you get the word out to parents. Parents need to know what you're doing with their money. Once they see the programs designed to support them and their children, they will open their wallets.

FINAL THOUGHTS

Idea Bank

Following is a list of miscellaneous ideas. Pick one that works for you and make it happen.

1. *Holiday Parties* Use any holiday such as May Day, Cinco de Mayo, President's Day (Washington & Lincoln), or Valentine's Day to have a party and charge admission. Make a potluck or order pizza and soda and charge an admission fee. Add a bake sale and a few games and you have a fundraiser. Negotiate with your pizza provider to give you a special rate. Domino's once donated to a Boy Scout Court of Honor because they valued the business from our scout families. For years, Domino's was the only place our family bought pizza.
2. *Flea Market Table* Have a table for your school at the flea market and sell white elephant items donated by the parents.
3. *White Elephant Store* Have a secondhand or white elephant store in the basement of the school, just as many churches do. Run it during the school year.
4. *Crafts Fair* Have a craft fair in the school just before Mother's Day. Offer crafts made by parents and children. Donate half the proceeds to the school and half to the maker of the items. Or donate 60 percent and keep 40 percent, whatever works for your school.
5. *Avon Calling* Get an Avon representative in the school to donate half her commission percentage and have an Avon Week in the school with the Avon lady taking orders and giving half her proceeds to the school.
6. *Candy* Sell candy at the flea market.
7. *Parent/Child Sporting Events* Have a father-daughter

volleyball game or a father-son basketball game or a teacher/student game or a parent/student tournament in the school. Charge a small participation fee. Serve food and have a bake sale at the event. Get corporations or fraternal organizations to sponsor so you can sell T-shirts commemorating the event and give out trophies to the winners. Keep the rest of the money for the school.

8. *Movie Theater Night* Get a movie theater to give your school a special discount price on tickets. Or rent and entire theater and have school night at the movies. Sell tickets at regular price and keep the difference for the school.

9. *School Play* At a school play, ask for donations, have a bake sale, sell popcorn and drinks.

10. Cash-In on Kindergarten

Put kindergarten parents in charge of an easy event with an experienced parent as co-chair to get the kindergarten parents involved quickly.

1. *Join Forces with the Girl Scouts* Make a deal with the Girl Scouts. Make an arrangement where kids sell Girl Scout cookies in the school for $3 per box; $2 go to the Girl Scouts and $1 goes to the parents association.

2. *Concerts for Cash* Any famous parents in your school? Any musicians? Back in the day, the classical musicians in our new kindergarten class got together and put on a concert in the school auditorium. They raised almost $5,000!

3. *Stand-Up Fund-raiser* Have a stand-up comedy night. With good publicity, you will attract aspiring comedians who are always looking for audience. Or have a kids' stand-up comedy night. Charge $5 admission.

4. *Halloween Village Art* Hold a Halloween window-painting contest. Get local merchants to donate the use of their

windows. Kids sign up to paint imaginative Halloween designs in water-based poster paint on the windows. Judge the windows and give out awards. Get a $10 registration fee from each child. Can't find prize donors? Give cash awards from the proceeds instead. This event takes place every year in Rye, New York. The local schools do not sponsor it, but the wonderful artwork is up for several weeks, keeping Halloween spirit alive. It's good publicity for the stores, too.

5. *Shovel Snow for Dough* Plan in advance to have a snow-shoveling day when your area's first snowstorm hits. Then, when it snows, you will be ready. Send middle and high school kids out to shovel driveways and shovel out cars. Charge $20 for a driveaway and $10 to dig out a car.

6. *Fashion Show* Have children or adults, or both, design and sew their own clothes and throw a fashion show. Provide donated refreshments. Charge $5 admission. This idea comes from the St. John's School in the United Kingdom.

7. *Cook Book* Create your own cookbook using recipes from the parents in your school. There are companies on the Internet, like www.fundcraft.com[1], that can produce a cookbook for your school.

8. *Pancake Breakfast* If you can commandeer your school cafeteria and kitchen, a pancake breakfast will be fun and raise money at the same time.

9. *Dog or Cat Show* Let children enter their pets. Have special ribbons for pet tricks. Make sure everyone gets a ribbon. Charge a $5 entry fee. Have a cat or dog "parade" where everyone can participate and an audience can cheer.

10. *Craft or Quilting-Making Contest or Fair* Award prizes for the best crafts or quilts. Charge and entry fee or a small admission fee to view the crafts. At the end of the show, sell any crafts the

---

1. http://www.fundcraft.com

makers want to donate to the school.

11. *Walkathon* Get sponsors, from your boss or grandma, to give $5 per mile walked. Conduct the walkathon with parents and children, or just children alone. You can raise money and get into good shape at the same time.

12. *Readathon* Suggested by the Parchment, Michigan, PA, a readathon is the same as a walkathon, only sponsors pay per book read. This is a long-term project, but you can create excitement and keep track of reading as it progresses.

13. *Pumpkin-Cooking Contest at Thanksgiving or Halloween* Charge and entry fee for all edibles made with pumpkin. From pies to casseroles, let your parents and kids run wild. Sell the entries after judging.

14. *Quiz Show* Conduct a Jeopardy-type game contest between parents and teachers, teachers and teachers, teachers and students, parents and students, or any other combination. Charge admission for those who wish to watch. Sell baked goods at intermission. This idea comes from the St. John's School in the United Kingdom.

15. *Start a Vegetable and Flower Garden on School Property* Let the kids plant and tend a small garden. Sell the vegetables and flowers at their own roadside stand when all is ripe and in full bloom.

16. *Your School's Day at the Ballpark* Approach a local minor league (or major league) baseball team about having a "day" for your school, when 20 percent of the box office receipts would go to your school.

17. *Art Show and Silent Auction* A silent auction of donated artwork, a free kid's art activity area, and a show of over 100 of Portland's artists, including a student gallery, coupled with some light fare from a local

18. bakery or the parents made up the Buckman Elementary and

DaVinci Arts Middle School's Art Show & Tell Portland, Oregon.

19. *Photo Sales* The enterprising parents of Oliver Middle School in Broken Arrow, Oklahoma, sold photos of memorable occasions, like awards ceremonies. Select a few gifted photographers from your parent body and do the same. Sell photos from the school play, graduation, class picnics, and other special school occasions.

20. *Keep Warm and Raise Money* Have throw blankets custom designed for your school by Liberty Logos, http://www.libertylogos.com/ Use your school colors, mascot, or logo. Finished size is 54"X 72". Perfect for a cold-weather fund-raiser.

1. *Looking for Just the Right Cookbook Company for your School?* Check out these companies:

- http://createmycookbook.com/
- https://www.morriscookbooks.com/
- http://cookbookfundraiser.com

1. *Try:* www.fund-raising.com[2]
2. *Fifth Grade Barbecue* Joseph Estabrook School in Lexington, Massachusetts, has a grade sponsor a barbecue to raise money.
3. *Market Day in Illinois* An Itasca, Illinois, a woman, Trudi Temple, started with day trips from suburban Illinois to Chicago's farmers' markets. Make a deal with local farmers' markets to come and sell for a fee in your school parking lot. A win/win situation: fresh, healthy food for all and money for the school and farmers, too!
4. *Bye-Bye Summer Sale* Have a secondhand kids' summer clothes sale in your school in October. People can donate shorts, T-shirts, and summer dresses that will be too small to wear next summer. They can buy summer clothes in a larger size ahead of time very inexpensively. This sale shouldn't deplete donations to the spring street fair where families donate outgrown winter clothes.
5. *An online ticket auction* Parents donate tickets to all sorts of events: movies, baseball games, concerts, museums, plays, any special event. Parents bid on the tickets online and pay that way as well. Once you get the donations, this is an easy event to run.
6. *Community partners* Contact local stores, from hardware to groceries and bakeries to restaurants. Issue frequent-buyer cards for the parents in your school. For every purchase made

2. http://www.fund-raising.com

by a parent in the school, the store will donate 5 or 10% of the purchase price to the school.

7. *Classes* Do you have parents who are experts at computers, yoga, Zumba, dancing, knitting, crocheting, sewing, acting, writing, or any other skill? Arrange for them to hold classes in the school in the evening. The PA can manage the classes, collect the money, and split the revenue with the parent who's conducting the class.

8. *Wrapping Paper* Buy extra wrapping paper. Sell it in your flea market around the holidays.

9. *A picnic basket auction* Each family puts together a picnic basket of goodies for a lunch in the park or even on school grounds. Put the baskets up for auction online. All monies paid for the baskets go to the parents association. Then have a picnic! (Do this in warm weather.)

CREATING NEW IDEAS

When brainstorming new ideas for your school, your most important resource is your intelligent, creative, devoted, hardworking parents. You will be surprised who comes up with the best ideas. A brainstorming session can get your fund-raising off the ground.

Run a brainstorming session as a business would; after all, fund-raising is a nonprofit business. Here is what you need to conduct a productive brainstorming session:

1. A large room you can occupy for at least four hours.
2. A huge pad of paper, an easel, and plenty of colored markers.
3. Chairs and table, preferably round so there is no "head," which often stifles people from speaking up.
4. Food—hungry people are more argumentative.
5. A board member with good or at least legible handwriting to chair the session or preferably two members: one to lead and one to write.
6. Creative people who are not afraid to speak up. When parents are part of the planning and idea-generating process, they are more likely to "own" the results and volunteer to move ideas forward.
7. You won't need many rules, but one is mandatory: no one is allowed to shoot down or criticize ideas. All ideas are acceptable, and all shall be heard. If you allow people to criticize or cut off ideas, before long no one will open their mouth and your meeting will be fruitless. The meeting leader should have a positive approach who can direct the meeting while still being open to new ideas. The leader should come in with some general topics to start off the session
8. Every new idea gets written on the pad. The leader asks people to expand on each idea. He or she must lead the

process when response is slow or people are shy. Call on people when necessary. Write down all the expansions on each idea and then tear off the sheet and clip, pin, or tape the sheet to the wall.

As the meeting progresses, the sheets will fill up the walls. The leader needs to assign ideas for follow-up to people in the meeting. When the meeting is over, the follow-up people take the big sheets with them. It's great if you can have a secretary in the meeting writing everything on a laptop so you have a record of all the ideas in another place in case someone's dog eats the big sheets, or the person in charge of follow-up, doesn't. Take pictures of the sheets with your cellphone so you have a back-up.

Follow-up is key. Without follow-up, a good idea is just a piece of paper. The fund-raising chair is responsible for all follow-ups. Ask the person who came up with the idea to head the committee to flesh it out and find a way to make it work.

Jump on the opportunity at the end of the meeting to assign a committee to each person who is taking home a big sheet. Try to convince the people who contributed to the big idea to be on the committee to make it happen. People work harder to make something they conceived a success.

DON'T GET DISCOURAGED!

If your fund-raiser doesn't live up to your expectations, don't give up. Your first fund-raiser will be your worst, since you will learn from it and make improvements that will get you better results the next time.

Each year your events will be bigger and better than the year before. Learn, tinker, fix, add, subtract, and make your events better. Keep going. The kids are counting on you.

GETTING VOLUNTEERS

Which brings me to the subject of volunteers. Fund-raising events happen only because somebody volunteers. Some people work tirelessly for years, others only bake a cake or supervise a class booth for an hour. Whatever the amount of time, the volunteers are the lifeblood of fund-raising.

HOW TO GET VOLUNTEERS

There are many ways to bring in volunteers. Here are a few that work for the schools across the country:

1. Post sign-up sheets on bulletin boards around school. This saves time.
2. Advertise the need for volunteers and describe the job thoroughly in your school newsletter.
3. Invite grandparents, aunts and uncles, too.
4. Ask every volunteer to bring a friend to the next meeting.
5. Have a special welcoming meeting on the first day of school for the new kindergarten parents. At this meeting, have board members and committee chairs speak briefly about what they do. Have sign-up sheets.

KEEPING VOLUNTEERS

Once you have volunteers, it's important to keep them. Getting volunteers is hard. You need to use patience, rewards, and acknowledgement to keep them coming back. You'll have smoothly running events with experienced people at the helm.

Volunteers who feel a sense of gratification and appreciation volunteer again. Following is a list of basic do's and don'ts when managing volunteers:

1. _Trust your volunteers._ That means you shouldn't look over the

shoulder of every volunteer to make sure he or she is doing a perfect job. Micromanaging your volunteers is a mistake. People leave if you watch them like a hawk. It's disrespectful.

2. *Make volunteering fun.* Have a few laughs, tell jokes, or relate funny stories while you work. Bring food, even if it's only a bowl of pretzels to nosh on while working. A volunteer who has a good time comes back.

3. *Acknowledge and appreciate.* Remember to use words of praise with your volunteers. Telling people they are doing a great job makes them want to come back and help again. Volunteers are hard to get, treat them well.

4. *Be positive.* Criticism just tears people down and drives them away. Everything doesn't have to be perfect.

5. *Be a good listener.* Be open to new ideas and ways of doing things. People who think their way is the only right way often end up doing everything by themselves. No one wants to work with a dictator. Besides, you never know where a good idea is going to come from. Don't shut people down with a negative attitude or you'll find yourself working alone.

6. *Listen to your volunteers.* When a volunteer complains that he or she needs help with a job, or additional tools, listen and be prepared to act. Either find someone to help her or him or else you jump in yourself. A volunteer who feels ignored, overworked, burned out, or overwhelmed won't come back again.

Here are several ways to reward volunteers:

1. *Throw a volunteer appreciation breakfast.* A few urns of coffee, some juice, and bagels with cream cheese are not expensive. Being invited to an appreciation breakfast makes your volunteers feel special. Make sure to go up to each and every volunteer and say thank you.

2. *Publish lists of volunteers for all your events in your school newsletter.* Seeing your name there is a real boost. People will see the same names over and over and a person's status in the school grows. Not to mention the fact that you know who doesn't mind volunteering and you can call people on one thank-you list to volunteer for another event.

3. *Purchase a "badge" of volunteering.* Order pins, like tie tacks, cute and colorful, with your school name and the word volunteer. It's a real prize, a sign of giving and belonging. You can get them cheaply from a premium company. Try: www.iprint.com[1], and www.epromos.com[2]

4. *Publish a list of volunteers on poster paper and hang it in the vestibule or office of the school.* Having your name on this list is a badge of honor.

CAVEAT:

Never create a "volunteer of the year award". By singling out one person for praise, you will make everyone else, who did even the smallest thing, feel unappreciated and second-rate. They may drop out leaving you losing volunteers instead of gaining.

Keeping volunteers is all about recognition, appreciation, listening, and laughing together. That's what makes fund-raising so special. It's a wonderful experience to get involved in your school. Be creative, laugh, and have a great time. Make a difference in your child's school. Your kids know that you care because you are there.

---

1. http://www.iprint.com

2. http://www.epromos.com

BUDGETING

Part of the job of raising the money is learning how to spend it. Creating and following a budget is an important part of running a parents association. You need to prepare a budget, present it, and have it approved by a majority vote.

The budgeting process starts with the creation of a budget committee. This should include at least: your treasurer, PA president, and fund-raising chair. Members of other important committees, like enrichment, who may be in charge of spending much of the money you raise, should also be on the committee.

The budget committee meets during the summer months to prepare a budget. The budget is presented to the parent body at a PA meeting as early in the school year as possible. Nothing can begin until that budget is approved.

WHAT IS A BUDGET?

A budget has two parts: income and expenses. Make a list of the estimated income from your fund-raising and a list of estimated expenses for the coming school year.

Once you've had some successful fund-raisers, you need to have a well-thought-out plan for the expenditure of the money. The first thing you do is take half the money and put it in a PA savings account. It earns interest while remaining untouched. If you place half your earnings in savings, before long you'll have a reserve fund. When you need to lay out money in advance, you can borrow it from the reserve fund. The reserve fund is essential. If you spend every penny you make, you'll never grow, as you won't have the necessary funds to lay out in advance for expanding events that will earn more money.

Every committee head who wants money for expenses should either be at the budget meeting or give his or her plans, in writing, to someone who will be at the meeting. It is not enough to say, "I want two thousand dollars for the health and safety committee."

Have a spending plan ready to explain, preferably in writing, and pass out to the members of the budget committee.

Plan on allocating money for the principal's discretion and some to teachers. Meet with the principal and discuss what he or she would do if they had more money. Budget what money you can toward his or her school enrichment plans.

Back in the day, we gave $200 to every teacher to spend on classroom supplies. For new teachers, the amount was $400. This allocation was spent by reimbursing teachers who spent the money and submitted invoices/bills to the PA. Please be prompt with reimbursement to the teachers. They do not have deep pockets to finance the enrichment of your child's classroom.

The treasurer needs to keep a close eye on expenditures, or your committees, principals, and teachers can go over budget by accident. Both the president and the treasurer of the PA should approve each principal and teacher reimbursement. Never budget your expenses to exceed your income. But you can budget to have money left over and not spend everything you raise.

Leftover funds can become an "opportunity budget." An opportunity budget is money available if some wonderful special opportunity should present itself to your school. For example, a traveling opera comes to town. Your principal makes a deal for the opera to perform at a cut-rate for the children in your school. But it will cost $500, and the principal has already spent his discretionary fund. With your opportunity budget, you have money to take advantage of this special event.

The budget should be re-examined in January. You will have had one or two fund-raising events by then and will have some idea if you have raised more or less than you budgeted. Some committees won't spend their full allotment—their budget can be reduced—and some may need more.

In January, revisit your earlier plans and make adjustments. Move money around as is necessary. Present the revised budget to the parents association for approval.

Your budget is your most important guideline. It'll help you focus your fund-raising efforts on specific needs. For example, if you are raising money for a new piano, music-loving parents might give more money than they would for a general fund-raiser. It will also tell you how well you're doing and where the most important school needs are.

Keep an open door for teachers. Some wonderful ideas have been created because money became available. Remember that as a member of the board of your parents association, you have a financial obligation to be responsible for the money that comes through your treasury.

CONTACT ME

Please share your fund-raising travails and triumphs, or ask me questions via email: jjoachim830@cs.com

IMPORTANT WEBSITES

WRAPPING PAPER
  Genevieve's: 1-800-842-6656
  MAGAZINES
  https://southwesternfundraising.com/family-reading-program/
  BOOK FAIR
  Scholastic: www.scholastic.com/bookfairs[1]
  KID'S GRAB BAGS
  The Oriental Trading Company:
  www.orientaltradingcompany.com[2]
  U.S. Toy Company: www.ustoycompany.com[3]
  T-SHIRTS
  www.iprint.com[4]
  www.epromos.com[5]
  www.vistaprint.com[6]
  CANDY SELLERS
  https://www.abcfundraising.com/
  www.allstarfundraising.net[7]
  www.fivestarfundraising.com[8]
  www.worldsfinestchocolate.com/start-fundraising/get-started[9]
  www.ezfund.com[10]

---

1.   http://www.scholastic.com/bookfairs

2.   http://www.orientaltradingcompany.com

3.   http://www.ustoycompany.com

4.   http://www.iprint.com

5.   http://www.epromos.com

6.   http://www.vistaprint.com

7.   http://www.allstarfundraising.net

8.   http://www.fivestarfundraising.com

9.   http://www.worldsfinestchocolate.com/start-fundraising/get-started

10.   http://www.ezfund.com

https://www.promotioninmotion.com/fund-raising/
SCHOOL STORE/LOGO ITEMS/PREMIUMS
www.discountmugs.com[11]
www.iprint.com[12]
www.epromos.com[13]
www.customprinting.com[14]
www.uscolorprint.com[15]
www.promotionalpencils.com[16]
www.thediscountprinter.com[17]
www.vistaprint.com[18]
CORPORATE WEBSITES
www.adoptaclassroom.com[19]
www.boxtops4education[20]
HIGH SCHOOL
Federal student college loans
https://studentaid.ed.gov/sa/fafsa

11.   http://www.discountmugs.com

12.   http://www.iprint.com

13.   http://www.epromos.com

14.   http://www.customprinting.com

15.   http://www.uscolorprint.com

16.   http://www.promotionalpencils.com

17.   http://www.thediscountprinter.com

18.   http://www.vistaprint.com

19.   http://www.adoptaclassroom.com

20.   http://www.boxtops4education

CPSIA information can be obtained
at www.ICGtesting.com
Printed in the USA
LVHW080605130120
643361LV00015BA/1073/P

9 781950 244577